THE LHASA MOON
TIBETAN COOKBOOK

THE LHASA MOON
TIBETAN COOKBOOK

by

Tsering Wangmo and Zara Houshmand

Illustrations by

Palden Choedak Oshoe, Zara Houshmand, Sidney Piburn,
Matthew Roberts, and Alison Wright

SNOW LION PUBLICATIONS

Ithaca, New York

Snow Lion Publications
P.O. Box 6483
Ithaca, New York 14851 USA
607-273-8519

ISBN 1-55939-104-9

Library of Congress Cataloging-in-Publication Data
Wangmo, Tsering, 1967-
The Lhasa Moon Tibetan cookbook / Tsering Wangmo, Zara Houshmand.
p.   cm.
ISBN 1-55939-104-9
1. Cookery, Tibetan. 2. Lhasa Moon (Restaurant). I. Houshmand, Zara.
TX 724.5.T55W35 1998
641.5951'5--dc21   98-39575   CIP

Printed in Canada

TABLE OF CONTENTS

❦   *Vegetarian dishes are indicated by this symbol*

SPECIAL THANKS

Shilo
Youlo Kelsang
Norbu Tenzin Norgey
Tsering Dolma (Nono)
Tashi Choden
Phurba Dolma (Mimi)
Sangye Tashi and Namkha Choden
Cheryl Haines
Colin Wright
Tibet Shop

INTRODUCTION

Ngotsa manang ne choe — "Eat shamelessly!"

Most first-time visitors to Lhasa Moon are very pleasantly surprised. Tibetan cooking is little known to the outside world, and what reputation it has is poorly served by travelers' experiences of a country under military occupation and a diet limited by the region's poverty and harsh climate. But the first and so far only Tibetan restaurant in San Francisco is changing that reputation, and it's a real discovery, even in this culinary world capital. Tsering Wangmo, the owner, chef, and guiding spirit of the place, offers her guests meals that are richly varied with both exotic surprises and the comforting "soul food" of Tibetan home cooking.

Tsering's family comes from the Kongpo Valley in eastern Tibet, and many of the dishes she learned from her mother show the influence of this fertile and forested region. Her family left Tibet like many thousands of other refugees fleeing the oppression and abuses of the Chinese occupation. Tsering was raised in Bylakuppe, an agricultural collective carved out of the South Indian jungle in the early 1960s by refugees unaccustomed to the heat and low altitude and with no experience of farming under such conditions. A naturally talented singer, she was sent to the Tibetan Institute of Performing Arts in Dharamsala, and spent several years there studying and performing the traditional opera, folk dances, and regional music of Tibet. Inspired by her own love of the arts she had learned, and the mission of preserving the culture that is being wiped out in Tibet itself, Tsering was determined to continue this work in the West. In 1989 she came to the U.S. and founded, along with Tashi Dhondup and Sonam Tashi, a small but fiercely dedicated and energetic troupe known as Chaksam-Pa, The Tibetan Dance and Opera Company.

At Lhasa Moon, Tsering offers another taste of Tibetan culture, though if you are lucky on a Saturday night you might also hear her sing. The dishes she serves are eclectic, and have been adapted for Western tastes. You will find less fat and more vegetarian choices than you would see in Tibet. The influence of a generation raised in exile in the refugee settlements in India is also unmistakable, where the hot climate demands lighter food, and a great variety of vegetables grow in the extreme humidity. Not only have many Indian dishes been appropriated by the Tibetans and adapted to suit their own tastes, but life in the settlements has changed their view of their own culture. Families originating in far-flung regions of Tibet are now close neighbors and are exposed to customs and cooking from beyond their native region. Likewise, the invisible walls separating the noble families of Lhasa from the common people have eroded under the pressures of exile, and dishes that were once exclusive to the aristocracy are becoming more widely known.

Traditional Tibetan Foods

In Tibet itself, the staple food is *tsampa*, roasted barley ground into flour and eaten as a paste moistened with tea. Of all grains, barley is the best able to withstand the cold high altitude and short growing season of Tibet. Wheat is a second main crop, eaten as bread or noodles, and rice is also grown along the southern borders of the country. After 1949, the Chinese government made a disastrous effort to convert vast areas of the country to intensive wheat farming by forcibly settling nomads and planting land that had formerly been used for grazing. The result was rapid erosion of the topsoil, miles of formerly fertile land made desert, and the first famines in Tibetan history. Until this time, the land had never failed to provide an adequate, if fragile, sustenance.

Much of Tibet's usable land can sustain only nomadic or semi-nomadic populations herding yak and sheep, living on a diet mainly of dairy and meat. The female yak, or *dri*, and the hybrid *dzo* produce a yellow milk that is much richer than cow's milk. It is diluted for drinking, and made into butter, yogurt, and various types of cheese. The butter, mixed in tea as a staple of the diet, is far more than food: it is accepted as currency for trade or taxes, burned for light in butter lamps, smeared on the face as an ointment for protection against wind and cold, and consumed medicinally. Except for a few wild roots, the nomads eat almost no vegetables at all.

The diet is much more varied in the villages and towns, and especially around Lhasa, the capital of Tibet, where a wide selection of vegetables is grown. Daikon, turnips, and peas are common, as are potatoes, onions, watercress, and similar greens. The most common fruits are pears, peaches, apricots, pomegranates, apples, and berries. Many of the fruits are preserved by drying, and walnuts are also grown.

The relative abundance of the Lhasa region has fostered a more elaborate local cuisine, influenced also by the concentration of noble families attached to the government and the city's attraction to pilgrims, scholars, and traders from other regions. Even in the relative isolation of Tibet before the Chinese occupation, Lhasa was the place where foreign customs were introduced and where fashions started. Muslim traders introduced curries from India, and the Lhasa aristocrats took to chopsticks and Chinese methods of steam cooking long before such things were known in the rest of the country. But there are other fertile areas besides

Lhasa with their own well-developed cooking styles. The Kongpo Valley, where Tsering's family hails from, is a forested region known for its many varieties of fruit. Amdo, where His Holiness the Dalai Lama was born, near the Chinese border, is known for its especially refined cooking style, and for the care, cleanliness, and enjoyment that Amdo cooks bring to their work.

Life in the Kitchen

The mother usually does most of a family's cooking, getting up before dawn to prepare the morning bread. Her daughters will help, and a mother will be happy if her firstborn child is girl. Children are given substantial responsibility for chores from the age of eight or nine.

Although important guests will be seated in the shrine room which serves as a formal living room, much of the women's social life happens in the kitchen, talking together as they work. Sitting on sacks of grain, they will use a simple table, or plastic spread on the ground, as the work surface. The warm heart of the kitchen is the stove built of mud-coated brick, rubbed and oiled till it shines, and protected by its own guardian spirit. The *tap-lha* kitchen spirit is fussy about cleanliness: if the milk boils over or you accidentally spill some food, you should offer a little barley flour to the spirit and ask for forgiveness as you toss the *tsampa* in the fire.

The stove is fueled by wood or dried yak dung resting on a metal grate, and bread is baked by burying it directly in the hot ashes in the stove. Three holes are cut into the top of the brick struc-ture, where cooking pots nestle. The fire is kept alive all day, for a cold stove is a sign of poverty. The kettle of buttered tea is refilled several times each day, pots of broth simmer slowly for hours, and at night the children may even sleep by the warmth of the stove.

The kitchen hearth is also the center of life in the nomads' home, a structure that is more like a house than a tent, protected from the wind by sod walls and divided into rooms by boxes stacked as partitions. The stove is built like a table, supported by two pairs of wild yak horns stuck upright in the earth.

Traditionally the pots and utensils—a few large ladles and strainers—were made of copper or brass, but now aluminum is common. A heavy cleaver and wooden chopping board are essential, as is a churn for mixing the buttered tea. The cooking pots are objects that carry special power and are handled with respect: one should never walk between pots resting on the floor, for example, but move around them or lift them up to pass. Such respect and appreciation for domestic objects is a familiar theme in Tibetan culture, and there are many folk songs that sing the praises of finely made but essentially humble objects.

Daily Meals

The entire household eats together, and servants or hired hands will generally share the meal with the family. Hospitality is offered easily, and travelers passing through will often be invited to join the family meal. The evening supper is usually the main meal of the day, though breakfast and lunch are also quite heavy. *Tsampa* can be eaten for breakfast, lunch, and dinner, though Tibetans raised in the settlements in India generally prefer rice and bread, and will usually eat *tsampa* for breakfast only. If not *tsampa* with tea, breakfast might be soup with bread. Lunch might consist of *tsampa* and dried meat, carried and eaten on a break while working in the fields. In India lunch is more likely to be rice and dal. Dinner is often *tukpa*, a hefty soup with meat and fresh noodles.

Before the Chinese occupation of Tibet, nearly a quarter of the male population lived in the monasteries. Their food, which might be grown on the monasteries' own lands or donated by local families, was extremely simple. The typical diet consisted of *tsampa* for breakfast, lunch, and dinner, often supplemented by a little dried yak jerky, and a lot of buttered tea. Monks who could afford it might occasionally fix themselves a bowl of noodle soup. The Tibetan monastic communities that have been reconstituted in India offer little better; the extreme poverty is mitigated by the Indian climate, which allows for slightly more variety. Breakfast is typically tea and bread; lunch is rice and watery dal; dinner is bread with a watery dish of vegetables and a small amount of meat in broth.

Considering the country's isolation and difficult terrain, Tibetans traditionally traveled a surprising amount, as traders, as nomads migrating seasonally, or as pilgrims who spent months en route to important shrines, doing prostrations as they went. The simplicity of the daily fare lends itself to easy meals on the road. The barley that is processed into *tsampa* is precooked, so it is virtually an instant meal: just add liquid. The cold dry climate is excellent for keeping food without refrigeration, and meat can be dried without a lot of salting. Cheese also is dried and easily carried, small pieces threaded on string like *mala* beads for counting prayers.

Celebrations

The dishes that Tsering serves at Lhasa Moon, and the recipes collected in this book, are far more interesting than the typical subsistence fare. As well as drawing on her experiences in India, Tsering has tapped her memories of celebration meals. A wedding feast can stretch for several days, as can elaborate picnics. You can build up an appetite dancing for hours, stamping feet in complex rhythms along with the strumming of the *danyen*. At weddings and festivals such as the Dalai Lama's birthday and at the springtime new year celebration, many of the special foods are considered auspicious: their very presence brings luck and signals prosperity.

Losar, the Tibetan lunar new year, is celebrated in February or March but preparations begin well in advance. Huge amounts of pastries are fried and an elaborate tower of confectionery in traditional shapes is constructed as an offering at the altar of the family's shrine in the best room of the house. A pot of wheat seeds is set to sprout, and the tender green shoots predict the abundance and prosperity of the year to come. A thorough spring cleaning culminates on the 29th day of the last month of the year, ridding the house of a year's accumulation of negative spirits. The kitchen is decorated with drawings—wishfulfilling jewels, suns and moons, conch shells, and other auspicious symbols to bring luck on the house.

The old year ends with a family meal of soup with fresh noodles cut from strips of dough. Several balls of dough also swim in the broth and one is served to each member of the family. Each contains a small object that reveals the recipient's true character or fortune for the coming year. Wood predicts long life, and heavy rock salt means laziness. Charcoal is for the mean-spirited, cotton for the kind-hearted, and chili for one whose "hot mouth" is quick to speak harsh words. Paper is fickle, easily swayed, but if your paper is inscribed with the sun, moon, or stars, you light up the darkness and make others happy.

After offerings and prayers, the new year begins with a special breakfast of hot mulled barley beer thickened with a little *tsampa* and sweetened with raisins. Later there is *desi*, sweet buttered rice that has been blessed at the monastery, and a feast that includes *pingsha* with long noodles for long life.

A high point of the celebration is the auspicious arrival of the Dekar, with his white-bearded mask and quick-witted songs. He will sing praises of the countryside and the towns, each as prosperous as a "pot full of noodles," as well as his own twisted version of Tibetan history, and then poke fun at his hosts, who hurry to offer him the best of their food and drink:

A great and compassionate gentleman said to me,
Dekar, don't get excited, be a little bit calm
  and collected.
Right now I will give you
enough meat and rice to stuff you,
sweet buttered rice like rolling eyes,
and noodle soup like swaying hips.
I will give you momos like a pleated chupa.
Wish-fulfilling Dekar, I will fill your mouth with fat!

Tibetans are very fond of picnics, which often last two or three days with much singing and dancing. White tents are pitched for shade and stacks of containers are filled with different foods which may be quite elaborate. Traditionally, the most festive of all picnic occasions was during the *Shoton*, the Yogurt Festival, actually an opera festival sponsored by Drepung Monastery at the end of their summer retreat. For several days, ritual dances alternated with musical dramas portraying magical adventures where the saintly protagonist always triumphed, but just barely, over a demonic queen or a treacherous minister. The audience would attend to their favorite parts, with much socializing on the fringes. In addition to the picnics brought from home, yogurt was served by the monks. Local farmers donated their surplus to the monastery and fresh milk and yogurt were abundant at the time of this summer festival.

Saka Dawa is also associated with special foods. This is the month when two of the most important events in the Buddha's life are celebrated on the same day, his birth and his passing into nirvana. Many people will avoid eating meat for the entire month, and fast on alternate days, or on the 10th and 15th days of the month. Much of the time is spent in prayer and doing prostrations, which burn a lot of energy; so on alternate days when not fasting, people eat yogurt, milk and rice, and the concoction known as *patsa maku*, noodles in a sauce of caramel, butter, and cheese.

Food and Ritual in Tibetan Buddhism

Westerners who are first introduced to Tibetan culture are often surprised that such devoutly Buddhist people are rarely vegetarian. The nomadic roots of the culture and the very climate of the land conflict uneasily with the ideals of Buddhism in this. Ever pragmatic, Buddhist teaching does not strictly prohibit eating meat, which is just as well in a country where so much of the land is suited only to grazing.

Tibetans will make varying degrees of effort to minimize the karmic damage of eating meat. Often the butcher's job is carried out by Muslims, of whom there are substantial communities in many towns. If a Buddhist must kill an animal, then prayers will be said in compassion for the animal. Animals that are intended for slaughter may be purchased and released as an act of merit. Sometimes a yak, sheep, or goat is consecrated to a particular deity. The animal is marked with tags of colored cloth in a special ceremony, and thereafter must not be harmed.

Larger animals are preferred as food, because a single one will feed many more people than a small animal. In this way, yak meat is best of all, but goat, mutton, and pork are still preferable to chicken or fish. Eating smaller creatures for pleasure would be unspeakably decadent: His Holiness the Dalai Lama has expressed his utter dismay at the loss of lives in a whole plateful of shrimp making a meal for a single person! The very idea of dropping a living creature into boiling water, even a lobster or crab, suggests witchcraft and demons.

At Lhasa Moon, Tsering has adapted many of the dishes to use chicken because so many Californians avoid red meat. But traditionally chicken is eaten only on rare occasions by villagers who keep hens for eggs. Fish is also rarely eaten, though it was always abundant in the lakes and rivers (a situation that has probably changed with the recent environmental destruction). Aside from religious considerations, the taste of fish is not much liked by many Tibetans. Fishing is strictly forbidden in the sacred lake that for generations has revealed images guiding the discovery of the Dalai Lama's rebirth.

In general, vegetarianism in Tibetan culture is not an all-or-nothing choice, but a range within the spectrum that moves towards purification. The so-called "black foods" are especially to be avoided by those who are meditating or engaging in purification practices: in addition to meat, the list includes garlic, onions, daikon, and eggs. People may choose to avoid meat during the month of Saka Dawa when the Buddha's birth and *parinirvana* are celebrated, or on the full and new moon of each month and other holy days. Or they may fast at such times.

At the far end of the spectrum are those yogis who fast extensively in extreme ascetic practices, perhaps living for months on nothing but water and three "meditation pills" a day. The pills are made chiefly of ground dried flower petals bound with a little honey and butter, but empowered by a special meditation that draws the nutritive essence from the environment into the pills. There are reports of one yogi near Lhasa who was subsisting on these pills alone when the Red Guard invaded, and therefore managed to defend himself successfully against their accusations that he was a parasite on society.

The use of food in Tibetan Buddhist rituals probably echoes customs that predate the arrival of Buddhism in Tibet. Food offerings are still dedicated to the local spirits of the land, a handful of *tsampa* tossed high in the air at a mountain pass, along with incense and a song of prayer. *Torma* are shapes molded out of *tsampa* and water that are fed to spirits. Colored with red dye, they may have their origin as a surrogate for animal sacrifices made in pre-Buddhist times. *Tsog* offerings are much finer, ritual feasts offered to the deities that protect the Dharma. A familiar sight on the altar are the conical mounds of *tsampa* mixed with butter and sugar to form a rich cookie dough, decorated with colored butter, and eaten after receiving the lama's blessing. Much has been written by anthropologists about food offerings used to bribe demonic spirits or to stimulate abundance through sympathetic magic. More simply, the giving and receiving of food is a very natural expression of relationship between living beings, and Tibetans live in very close relationship with the spirits that surround them, both supernatural and natural. Even the final disposal of one's corpse in the infamous "sky burial" is conceived as an act of feeding other creatures.

In his autobiography *Freedom in Exile*, His Holiness the Dalai Lama speaks of his attachment as a child to the monastery's Master of the Kitchen, commenting, "I sometimes think that the act of bringing food is one of the basic roots of all relationships." And the connection between giving food and understanding the interrelationship of all life is recognized also in stories about the belated discovery of an enlightened master who lived humbly as a monastery cook; or the stories of a great lama who gathers his disciples to test their progress, only to discover that the most highly realized of all is the cook, who has neither meditated nor studied, but simply served the others.

May you have long life,
may the house be filled with grain,
and may you have the luck
to make use of this abundance.

—Tibetan drinking song

Ingredients and Amounts

Most of the recipes here will serve four people, more or less. The exceptions are a few foods that are more easily made in large amounts for parties or for keeping.

Most of the ingredients used in Tibetan cooking are readily available in the West. Very few are harder to locate but can be found in Asian markets in most cities. Almost nothing is indispensable, and substitutions are suggested in the recipes.

We have included instructions for some very basic Tibetan foods that are generally unobtainable in the West, such as *tsampa* flour, cheeses, and barley beer. You can easily enjoy the best of Tibetan cooking without these more ambitious production processes, but if you are so inclined, the methods are practical for a modern kitchen and the results authentic.

Many of the dishes call for chopped beef. Ideally you should mince the beef finely by hand using a heavy cleaver. If you have a food processor, this also works well. Otherwise you can use ground beef, but it tends to lose its juices and dry out easily, in comparison to meat chopped by hand.

Spices are usually ground fresh for use with a stone mortar and pestle. The most commonly used spices are chilies of various types, fresh garlic and ginger, *emma*, and turmeric. Tsering uses paprika in many of the dishes at Lhasa Moon. It is less commonly used in Tibet but we find it adds depth to the flavor without changing the basic character of the dishes. Tsering often adds red peppers for color accent, and almost any Tibetan dish benefits from chopped cilantro or green onions sprinkled on top. However, when preparing several dishes for the same meal, these garnishes and the optional paprika should be varied so that all the dishes are not the same.

Daikon

Daikon, the large white Japanese radish, is used in many of the recipes. They are best when very firm, crisp, and juicy. Avoid soft, rubbery ones or any with wrinkled skin, but if necessary you can freshen a wilted daikon by soaking it in cold water for an hour. Long, slow cooking makes the daikon very juicy, and Tsering claims they are not properly done until the flesh has darkened slightly and turned translucent throughout. However the color change seems to depend on the freshness of the daikon and the color of the cooking liquid. It may not be obvious when cooking very fresh daikon in a vegetable broth. If you cannot find fresh daikon, turnips are a good alternative in cooked dishes.

Droma

Droma is the small clusters of sweet roots of potentilla, which grows on hillsides and in woods, and is hard to come by unless you can go foraging in the wild and know what to look for. It has a subtle flavor rather like sweet potato, which can be used as a substitute. However, *droma* holds its shape better and does not become as soft as sweet potatoes when fully cooked. It is used in the ceremonial sweet rice called *desi,* and is also cooked simply with butter.

Emma

Emma is the Tibetan name for the dried berries of various species of the prickly ash shrub, *Zanthoxylum.* Known as "Sichuan pepper" (*hua jiao* in Mandarin), it is readily available in Asian groceries. There is no worthwhile substitute, but the flavor is subtle and you can omit it without significantly changing the character of a dish. Like all spices, *emma* is best if ground fresh just before you use it. It need not be ground very finely and you can crush it easily in a mortar and pestle, or even with the back of a spoon in small bowl. Tibetans believe that *emma* destroys the toxins in meat that is slightly off.

Garam Masala

Indian *garam masala*, a mixture of spices, is sometimes used in Tibetan curries and in local dishes that have been adopted by the refugee communities in India. A typical *garam masala* can be made with 2 oz. coriander seed to 1 oz. each of cumin, black pepper, cardamom pods, bay leaf, cinnamon, and cloves. Roast the coriander and cumin seeds and peel the cardamom after measuring it. Then grind all the spices together and store in an airtight container.

Ginger

Ginger is always used fresh, never dried. Measurements are given as the length of a piece cut from a medium-sized root. The ginger is usually chopped very finely or sometimes just crushed with the back of a knife, and need not be peeled.

Ping

Ping are thin transparent noodles, quite firm in texture, made from bean flour. They are widely available at Asian markets. The best *ping* noodles are those made from mung beans, but green bean noodles (*sai fun*) are also good. Rice noodles look similar, but are too mushy when cooked. Italian vermicelli is a reasonable substitute, but it should be boiled according to the package directions rather than soaked.

The noodles are packaged in small bundles which may vary in size depending on the manufacturer. We have specified 2 oz. bundles, but you may need to adjust if your *ping* is packaged differently. Soak the noodles in hot, not boiling, water for 15–20 minutes before adding to other ingredients. Hot tap water is hot enough. Make sure there is enough water to keep the noodles covered as they expand.

Tibetan Names

Many of the dishes included in this book are well-known to any Tibetan, though the names may vary with regional dialects. Other names simply describe the main ingredients, particularly for dishes Tsering has invented.

The Tibetan terms used in this book have been rendered in English following Tsering's own pronunciation as closely as possible. Food hardly seems an appropriate subject to delve into the complexities of Tibetan spelling, which differs widely from current pronunciation. Unfortunately, most restaurant menus use an unhelpful hybrid of pronunciation and transliteration.

Vegetarian Dishes

In addition to the section devoted to vegetable dishes, you will find other meatless dishes throughout the book marked 🍎.

Soups

We have included in this section lighter soups that serve well as the first course of a meal. Under *Noodle Dishes (Tukpa)*, pages 47-60, you will find many other heartier soups that are complete meals in themselves.

A light soup is sometimes served as part of a more elaborate meal in the homes of the aristocracy, but most Tibetans will eat soup for breakfast. It is usually accompanied by a wheat bread or the *tsampa* dough called *pa*, both of which are often squeezed into a hollow spoon shape that is used to scoop up the soup before eating the soaked dough. In India, rice often replaces the bread or *tsampa*.

Cheese Soup

Churu

The mixture of hot chili with the pungent, mold-ripened *churu* cheese, after which the soup is named, is a uniquely Tibetan combination of flavors. Blue cheese makes a good substitute for *churu*.

This recipe is popular in the region of Kongpo, where it is usually eaten for breakfast with *tsampa* dough.

INGREDIENTS:

½ onion, chopped
oil for frying
1 tomato
1 jalapeño chili
2 tablespoons blue cheese or *Churu,* page 118
¼ lb. chopped beef
¼ teaspoon paprika (optional)
¼ teaspoon garlic, chopped
¼ teaspoon fresh ginger, chopped
¼ teaspoon ground *emma* (Sichuan pepper)
5 cups water
¼ cup cornstarch

Fry the onion in oil till brown and soft. Add the paprika, garlic, and ginger and fry briefly. Add the meat, stirring constantly, and then add the chili just before the meat is fully cooked. Turn the heat down low and add the cheese. When the cheese has melted, add the tomato and water. Mix the cornstarch in a little extra water (about ¼ cup) and pour it into the soup while stirring. Bring to the boil while stirring and remove from the heat as soon as the soup has thickened slightly.

Roasted Potato Soup 🍎

Shogo Tang

This soup is best when the potatoes are roasted in the ashes of the cooking fire. You can reproduce the smoky flavor by broiling the potatoes until they are slightly charred. Don't use a blender or the mixture will be gummy.

INGREDIENTS:

3 potatoes (use large waxy potatoes or smallish baking potatoes)
1 tablespoon butter
1 inch fresh ginger, chopped
4 cloves garlic, chopped
4–5 dried red chilies, crushed
¼ teaspoon ground *emma* (Sichuan pepper)
4–5 cups water, broth, or Tibetan tea
1 green onion, chopped

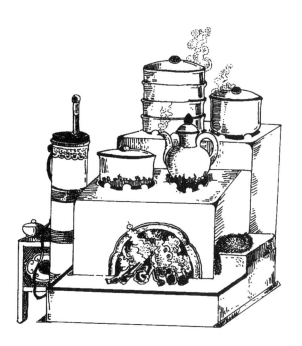

Broil the potatoes until brown and slightly charred, turning once. This will take about 40 minutes. When they are done, and cool enough to handle, peel them and chop the skins.

Fry the garlic, ginger, chili, and *emma* together in butter in a soup pot. Add the potatoes and chopped potato skins, and mash them with the spices, adding the liquid gradually. The potatoes should be slightly chunky. Heat thoroughly, stirring to prevent sticking.

Sprinkle chopped green onion on each serving.

Roasted Eggplant Soup 🌱

Duluma Jen

Eggplant does not grow in Tibet, but it is very common in India. This recipe, from the Tibetan settlement at Bylakuppe in southern India, shows how traditional cooking methods have been adapted for the unfamiliar produce found by the Tibetans in exile. Very similar in technique to the traditional *Shogo Tang* (Roasted Potato Soup, page 23), the smoky flavor suits the eggplant very well and stands up to the fierce heat of the chilies. "We sweat when we eat this!" says Tsering, who uses half a cup of chili for four people, but a more subtle version with less chili is also very good.

INGREDIENTS:

3–4 Japanese eggplants, or 1 large globe eggplant
1 tablespoon butter
1 inch fresh ginger, chopped
4 cloves garlic, chopped
4–5 dried red chilies, crushed
¼ teaspoon ground *emma* (Sichuan pepper)
1 tomato
4–5 cups water, broth, or Tibetan tea
1 green onion, chopped

Cut Japanese eggplant in half lengthwise or globe eggplant in ½-inch slices. Brush the cut sides with a little melted butter. Broil until brown and slightly charred, turning once.

Remove the charred skins from the eggplant and grind the flesh briefly in a blender or mortar and pestle. If you use a blender, add 1 cup of the water, broth, or tea to blend easily. It is best if still slightly lumpy, with a few flecks of skin remaining.

Fry the garlic, ginger, chili, and *emma* together in butter in a soup pot. Chop the tomato and add it to the fried mixture along with the eggplant. Continue cooking, stirring constantly, for 2 minutes. Stir in the remaining liquid and heat through.

Sprinkle chopped green onion on each serving.

Corn Soup 🎔

Ashom Tang

Corn soup is popular in Dharamsala, served with slight variations at many of the cafes and restaurants that cater to travelers in this colorful mountain town that is the heart of the Tibet community in exile.

INGREDIENTS:

½ onion, chopped
1 tablespoon butter
¼ teaspoon paprika
1 clove garlic, finely chopped
½ inch fresh ginger, finely chopped
1 tomato, chopped
1 square (12 oz.) firm tofu
3 cobs fresh corn and 1 tablespoon cornstarch,
    or 1 15-oz. can creamed corn and ½ cup frozen
    (or canned) whole kernel corn, drained
4 cups water
1 green onion, chopped

Sauté the onion in butter or oil in a soup pot until brown and soft. Add the paprika, garlic, and ginger and cook briefly. Add the tomato and the tofu, cut into small cubes, along with the water. If using fresh corn, cut it from the cob and add it to the pot, along with the cornstarch mixed in a little extra water. If using canned and/or frozen corn, add them both now. Bring to a boil, and simmer for a minute, stirring to prevent sticking.

Sprinkle chopped green onion on each serving.

Milarepa's Nettle Soup 🌱

Sabtuk

The story of the twelfth-century saint Milarepa holds a special place in the hearts of Tibetans. Wronged by greedy relatives, he studied magic to wreak vengeance. The effect was so spectacularly successful that remorse moved him to seek enlightenment, suffering endless ordeals to prove his devotion to his teacher. His legacy includes the hundreds of Dharma poems that he composed extemporaneously, still sung today with the simple and powerful beauty of folksongs.

Milarepa's ascetic practices included a diet of nettles, remembered in this soup from western Tibet. The toxin that causes nettles to sting is destroyed by cooking. The leaves are rich in iron and vitamin C, and also contain protein.

In Dharamsala, if you wake up early you might see elderly women using small metal tongs or scissors to pick nettles by the roadside, choosing the smallest, most tender leaves from the top of the plant. Early morning is the best time, of course, to avoid running into neighbors who turn up their noses at the idea of eating weeds.

INGREDIENTS:

6 cups broth or water
1 inch fresh ginger, finely chopped
3–4 cloves garlic, finely chopped
¼ teaspoon ground *emma* (Sichuan pepper)
1 lb. nettle leaves
salt to taste

Boil the broth or water with the ginger, garlic, and *emma*. Fill another pot with water and bring it to the boil. Dump the nettles into the boiling water to blanche them for a moment. Remove from the heat and immediately drain the nettles, squeezing out any excess water. Chop the greens and add them to the spiced broth. Let it boil again for a few minutes and add salt to taste.

SNACKS AND APPETIZERS

Tibetans do not normally serve appetizers as a separate course at the beginning of a meal. They do, however, offer guests an assortment of nibbles, which may or may not precede a meal. The selection might include candies, fresh or dried fruits such as apricots and raisins, nuts, and dried meat. The snacks may be served in small dishes or presented in a *loma*, a flexible hand-woven basket with a tight-fitting lid which is also used for carrying dry foods for picnics or offerings.

Many of the dishes included in this section evolved at Lhasa Moon in response to Westerners' requests for appetizers. Others are favorite Tibetan snacks and street foods. Any of the stuffed dumplings called *Momos*, pages 37-44, and Beef or Vegetable Pastries, pages 45-46, also make excellent appetizers, especially for a party.

Beef Jerky

Sha Kampu

Usually made from yak meat, air-dried jerky is a common method of preserving meat in Tibet. It may be served as a snack or with some *tsampa* as a simple main meal, and it makes an easy travelers' meal. The salt in the soy sauce acts as a preservative, so don't omit it or substitute a different type of sauce.

You can make the strips very long by cutting the meat continuously in a zigzag pattern. You may need a second person to hold the meat while you cut it.

INGREDIENTS:

2 lbs. top round beef
½ cup soy sauce
1½ teaspoons chili powder
1 tablespoon garlic, finely chopped

Cut the meat into long thin strips, half an inch wide. Mix the soy sauce, chili, and garlic together in a bowl. Dip the meat in the mixture to coat it thoroughly. Arrange the strips on wire clothes hangers or hang them directly from a clean string, stretched across a warm, dry, airy place where they can remain undisturbed. A sunny window works well. Leave the meat to hang for two to three days, until it is dry and brittle enough to break into pieces. Store in an airtight container.

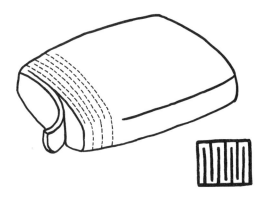

Spicy River Fish

Nya Taba

Fish is rarely eaten in Tibet, although it is sometimes recommended as a remedy for back pain. In the Tibetan settlements in India, fish is regarded as an expensive delicacy and is available only once a week on market days.

This particular method of preparing fish is the specialty of a street seller in the small town of Kangra, where performers from the Tibetan Institute of Performing Arts would stop regularly when touring to the refugee settlements. They say the spicy fish keeps them alert on the road and prevents car sickness.

The fish used in Kangra is similar to trout, but a less delicate fish would work just as well, if not better. Of course, if you use a large ocean fish like tuna you can choose a cut that avoids the bones.

INGREDIENTS:

1 lb. fish, cleaned weight
¼ cup soy sauce
1 teaspoon garlic, finely chopped
1 teaspoon fresh ginger, finely chopped
1 teaspoon paprika
¼ teaspoon ground *emma* (Sichuan pepper)
2 teaspoons ground dry red chili
oil for deep frying

Gut the fish and cut off the head, but don't remove the skin. Cut the fish into slices 2 inches wide. Mix the soy sauce and spices to make a marinade, and add the fish slices. Allow the fish to marinate overnight; if you leave it just a few hours, the flavor remains on the skin only.

Heat the oil in a small deep pan. Fry the fish in small batches so the oil stays hot. Each batch should take roughly 2 minutes to cook, perhaps less if the pieces are smaller. Test by cutting a piece open to see if the fish is flaky.

Pancakes with
Bean Thread and Vegetable Filling ❦

Ping Alla

Tsering invented this dish at the restaurant to satisfy the Western desire for appetizers, which are rarely eaten in Tibet. The pancakes are inspired by spring rolls but are healthier as they use much less oil.

This recipe will make six pancakes, enough for six people as an appetizer or four as a light meal. You can omit the eggs from the pancake batter if you wish, but in that case you must let the batter sit overnight or it will be very difficult to handle.

BATTER INGREDIENTS:

2 cups flour
1 teaspoon baking powder
2 eggs
2 cups water

Mix all the ingredients well. Let the batter sit at least half an hour, and ideally overnight.

FILLING INGREDIENTS:

1 bunch (2 oz.) bean thread noodles
¼ lb. shitake or other mushrooms
½ onion, chopped
oil for frying
½ teaspoon garlic, chopped
½ teaspoon fresh ginger, chopped
⅛ teaspoon salt
2 cups cabbage, thinly sliced
1 carrot, cut into slivers

Soak the noodles in enough hot water to cover them as they swell, for 20–30 minutes. If you are using shitake, cut them in ½-inch thick slices. If you are using other mushrooms, slice as thinly as possible.

Fry the onion till brown with the garlic, ginger, and salt. If you are using shitake, add them now, stir-frying till they just wilt. Add the cabbage and carrot, stir-frying till heated through but still quite crisp.

If you are using other mushrooms, fry them separately from the rest of the filling with a little oil and salt until they are brown, and add them to the filling at the end.

Drain the noodles and cut through the pile a few times with a scissors to make the lengths more manageable. Toss the noodles with the rest of the filling.

Heat a nonstick omelet pan over medium heat. Brush the hot surface lightly with oil, and immediately pour in ⅙ of the batter (⅔–¾ cup). Swirl the pan around to coat it with the batter. When the pancake is golden brown on the bottom and covered with small holes on the top, flip it to finish cooking the other side.

Spread ⅙ of the filling in a line across the middle of each pancake and roll it up. You can serve them whole or slice them into bite-size pieces. Serve with the chili sauce called *Sonam Penzom Sibeh*, page 121, using the version without yogurt.

Daikon Slices 🌱

Labtak

This dish was created by Gyatso, Tsering's first partner in the restaurant. After a night of partying, too much *chang*, and a feast of lamb and daikon stew, the only food left in the morning was a little of the stewed daikon. Frying the slow-cooked daikon in butter resulted in a very subtle taste and juicy texture.

This is also excellent as a side dish with roast lamb or beef. Choose daikon that is very crisp and fresh.

INGREDIENTS:

1 lb. daikon
1 lb. beef bones, or 1 onion and 1 tomato
1/8 teaspoon whole *emma* (Sichuan pepper)
2 inches fresh ginger, crushed
4–5 cloves garlic
1/2 teaspoon salt
1 tablespoon butter

Cut the daikon into 3/4-inch slices and place it in a deep pot. Add the beef bones, or the tomato and onion, cut into quarters. Cover with water and add the *emma*, ginger, garlic, and salt. Bring to a boil over high heat and then turn the heat low to simmer for about 1 hour.

Remove the daikon from the broth, which can be kept for soup. Heat the butter in a frying pan till it just begins to brown and add the daikon. Turn the heat down and fry the daikon slices till they brown, turning to cook the other side.

Serve with the chili sauce called *Sonam Penzom Sibeh*, page 121, using the version without yogurt.

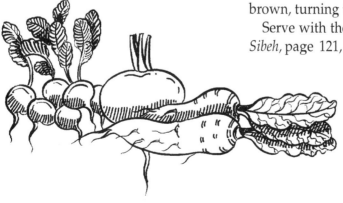

Mung Bean Gelatin 🌱

Le-ping

This is a very popular snack, sold on the street and often at public teachings and initiations. The women of Lhasa are said to make the best *le-ping* in Tibet. The smooth, cool texture and spicy heat are an acquired taste but one that becomes addictive, prompting city walks in search of a *le-ping* seller.

You can serve *le-ping* with any chili sauce or, in the style of the street sellers, let each person make their own sauce by sprinkling with a selection of seasonings. This can include, in any proportion you like, soy sauce, vinegar, crushed dried chili, and garlic water, which is made by crushing fresh garlic and covering it with a little water. Traditionally you would place the *le-ping* in a small covered container with the seasonings, and shake it to mix the sauce.

Mung bean flour is available in Korean markets, sometimes labeled "green bean flour." The flour itself should be white, not the yellow or green types sometimes found. The garlic and chives in this recipe are Tsering's own addition. They add flavor and look pretty suspended in the gelatin.

INGREDIENTS:

1 cup mung bean flour
4 cups water
3–4 cloves garlic, finely chopped
6–7 leaves chives, chopped
salt to taste

Bring the water to a boil and then turn the heat down low. Mix the mung bean flour with just enough extra water to make a pourable paste, just as you would use cornstarch. Add the flour mixture slowly to the boiling water while stirring quickly. Stir in the garlic, chives, and salt.

Pour the mixture into lightly oiled muffin tins or a rectangular pan. It should be about 1 inch deep. (A standard 7½ x 11¾-inch pan works well.) Let it stand at room temperature until set, about 5 hours. If you refrigerate it to hurry the process it will turn milky and lose its fresh, transparent look.

Cut into 2-inch squares, or serve individual rounds if using muffin tins. You can pre-mix the sauce and pour a spoonful over each serving, or mix your own at the table.

Fried Pork Ribs

Paksha Tsima

These bite-sized pieces of crisp-fried pork ribs are good finger food for parties. Ask the butcher to cut the ribs for you into one-inch pieces.

INGREDIENTS:

2 lbs. pork spare ribs, cut into 1-inch pieces
1/4 cup soy sauce
1/4 teaspoon garlic, finely chopped
1/4 teaspoon ginger, finely chopped
1 teaspoon paprika
1/4 teaspoon ground *emma* (Sichuan pepper)
1/2 teaspoon ground chili
vegetable oil for deep frying

Mix the soy sauce and spices. Add the ribs and mix by hand to coat each piece. Let the ribs sit in the marinade for at least half an hour, and preferably overnight.

Pour vegetable oil in a pan to a depth of 1 1/2 inches, and heat. Using chop sticks or tongs, take the meat directly from the marinade a few pieces at a time and fry in the oil. Watch the oil, as it will splatter fiercely. Be careful not to crowd the pieces. Turn them over to cook both sides until brown, about 2–3 minutes.

Serve with any chili sauce.

Crispy Chicken Bites

Chasha Katsa

This is a variation of *Paksha Tsima* using chicken instead of pork, one of Tsering's creations for Lhasa Moon.

Thigh and leg meat are best for this dish; breast is too dry. Tibetans prefer the meat on the bone, but cutting the bones properly takes some experience and a heavy cleaver, and even so, you will have sharp pieces to deal with. You may prefer simply to cut the meat off the bone.

INGREDIENTS:

1 lb. boned chicken, or 1½ lbs. with bones
¼ cup soy sauce
1 tablespoon plain yogurt
¼ teaspoon garlic, finely chopped
¼ teaspoon ginger, finely chopped
1 teaspoon paprika
¼ teaspoon ground *emma* (Sichuan pepper)
vegetable oil for deep frying

Cut the chicken into bite-sized cubes. Mix the soy sauce, yogurt, and spices. Add the chicken and mix by hand to coat each piece. Let the chicken sit in the marinade for at least half an hour, and preferably overnight.

Pour vegetable oil in a pan to a depth of 1½ inches, and heat. Using chop sticks or tongs, take the meat directly from the marinade a few pieces at a time and fry in the oil. It will splatter fiercely. Be careful not to crowd the pieces. Turn them over to cook both sides until brown, about 2–3 minutes.

Serve with any chili sauce.

Cabbage Salad 🍎

Tangtse

The name *tangtse* literally means "cold vegetable." This is the only real salad known in traditional Tibetan cooking. It is a refreshing complement to *momos,* and works well as a side dish with any main course.

INGREDIENTS:

½ white cabbage
1 daikon
1 carrot
juice of 1 lemon
1 teaspoon salt
1 teaspoon ground chili (optional)

Slice the cabbage very thinly, as you would for cole slaw. Cut the daikon and carrot into very fine julienne strips, or grate them coarsely. Toss the vegetables with the lemon juice, salt, and chili until well mixed.

Stuffed Dumplings (Momo)

Making *momos* is a lot of work;
Eat too much and your stomach will hurt.
—*Tibetan rhyme*

If there is a single dish that represents Tibetan food, it is *momos*. These steamed packets of filled pasta are universally loved, and served both for ordinary meals and at almost every party. There is one exception—*momos* are never eaten on the first day of the new year, because the meat closed up in dough would signify a shutting off of good luck.

Making *momos* is labor intensive, but the activity is often the heart of the party, with many hands working together. The men usually do the chopping of the meat and the women shape the *momos*, with much gossip and dirty jokes to lighten the work.

All the subtleties of *momo*-making technique are aimed at keeping the little packets of filled dough as juicy as possible. For this reason the meat is chopped rather than ground, the vegetables are handled very lightly, and the *momos* must not be overcooked. There are also subtle techniques in-

volved in eating *momos*. The connoisseur first bites a small hole in the dough and sucks out the juice, then spoons chili sauce into the hole and eats the rest. You can serve *momos* with any chili sauce but *Sonam Penzom Sibeh*, page 121, is best.

Basic Momo Dough

This amount will serve four as a main course, or eight as an appetizer.

> 2½ cups flour
> ¾ cup water

Mix the flour and water into dough, and knead it well. The amount of water needed may vary slightly depending on the age of the flour. The dough should be as moist as for ordinary bread. Cover the dough and set it aside to rest while preparing the *momo* filling.

Shaping Momos

Knead the dough until it becomes elastic. Keep the surface of the dough, your hands, and the work table well floured. Roll the dough under your palms to a long cylinder about one inch in diameter. Break off balls of dough, each about one inch in diameter.

Roll each ball in your palms to make a smooth sphere and then press to flatten it into a small circle. Use a floured rolling pin to enlarge the circle, working in a circular motion around the edges so that the middle remains slightly thicker.

If you are making more than one type of filling, use different shapes to tell them apart. The round *momos* are the prettiest, but the longer shapes are easier to eat without losing the juices. The monks' *momos* are so named because they are the easiest and quickest to make, and therefore the preferred shape when making vast numbers to feed a monastery.

For all shapes, begin by holding the circle of dough in your left hand and place a tablespoon of filling in the center.

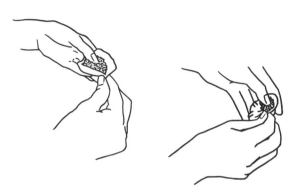

If you are familiar with making filled pastries to be baked, you'll find that the *momo* dough stretches to accommodate more filling than you would expect. Vegetable *momos* especially should be filled quite tightly, as the filling will shrink when it cooks. Also, you don't need to moisten the edges of the dough to make them stick.

Monks' Momos

Use your thumb and forefinger to pinch a small fold in the edge of the circle. Continue pinching the two edges flat together, working your way around the half-circle. With your other thumb, keep pushing the filling in towards the center. Finish with a single pinch at the top.

Round Momos

Use your thumb and forefinger to pinch a small fold in the edge of the circle. Then, leaving the thumb in the same position, gather another pinch of dough from the outside edge with your forefinger. Keep repeating this motion, occasionally using your other thumb to push the filling in towards the center. The pinched edge will form a spiral, gradually closing down to a tiny hole that you can pinch shut. When the shape is complete, press the sides lightly to puff it up.

Crescent Momos

Use your thumb and forefinger to pinch a small fold in the edge of the circle. Continue pinching the two edges together, but with each pinch, fold a pleat in the outside edge. With your other thumb, keep pushing the filling in towards the center. You can leave the crescent shape as is, or pinch the two ends together to form a circle if you need another shape to distinguish different fillings.

How to Cook Momos

Momos were originally baked, buried in the hot ashes of the cooking fire in a mud-brick hearth, and you can still find them cooked this way in the villages and tents of rural Tibet. Cooking in steam is a fairly recent introduction, influenced by Chinese cooking and established first, as most fashions were, in Lhasa. If you are purist enough to bury your *momos* in ashes, then you should also use authentically fatty cuts of meat for the filling, and probably not bother with vegetable *momos*.

Otherwise, arrange the *momos* on a lightly oiled steamer tray. You can fit them as close together as you like, so long as they do not touch. Bring the water to a boil before placing the tray of *momos* in the steamer.

Steam meat *momos* for 10 minutes at most, and vegetable *momos* for 5–7 minutes. Spinach *momos* need only 4 minutes as the filling is precooked. Be careful not to overcook the *momos*. Test them by opening the steamer and touching the dough lightly with a fingertip. The dough will no longer be sticky when done.

You can make *momos* in advance and freeze them for later use. Do not defrost them; just place the frozen *momos* in the steamer. Allow 15 minutes for frozen meat *momos*, and 10–12 minutes for frozen vegetable *momos*.

Momos can also be cooked in a soup called *Motuk*, pages 53-54.

Beef Momo Filling

Sha Momo

Tibetans often prefer cheaper cuts of meat because the extra fat adds flavor. Chopping the meat by hand makes the *momos* juicier, but you can use ground beef if you are in a hurry. The celery is not traditional, but is Tsering's addition to make the dish lighter.

INGREDIENTS:

1 lb. beef
1 large onion, finely chopped
2 inches fresh ginger, finely chopped
4 cloves garlic, finely chopped
½ teaspoon ground *emma* (Sichuan pepper)
⅓ cup green onion or chives, chopped
1 teaspoon oil
¼ cup water
3 stalks celery, finely chopped
¼ teaspoon salt

Chop the meat very finely, unless you are using ground beef. Mix it thoroughly with all the other ingredients.

Fill the *momos* and steam for 10 minutes.

Chicken Momo Filling

Chasha Momo

Chicken is not traditionally used for *momos* in Tibet, but this is a favorite at the restaurant for Americans who don't eat red meat. Don't use ground chicken, or the *momos* will be mushy.

INGREDIENTS:

1 lb. boneless chicken
1 large yellow onion, finely chopped
2 inches fresh ginger, finely chopped
4 cloves garlic, finely chopped
1/2 teaspoon ground *emma* (Sichuan pepper)
1/3 cup chives, chopped
1 teaspoon oil
1/4 cup water
3 stalks celery, finely chopped
1/4 teaspoon salt

Chop the chicken very finely by hand. Mix it thoroughly with all the other ingredients.

Fill the *momos* and steam for 10 minutes.

Vegetable Momo Filling 🌶

Tse Momo

Vegetable *momos* are rarely made in Tibet, although you can sometimes find very heavy, doughy potato *momos*. This recipe was invented at one of the Tibetan farming settlements in south India, where meat is an expensive luxury.

INGREDIENTS:

½ bunch celery
½ small cabbage
1 bunch spinach
1 bunch green onions
1 tablespoon oil
1 large yellow onion, finely chopped
1 ½ teaspoons garlic, finely chopped
1 teaspoon fresh ginger, finely chopped
½ teaspoon paprika
¼ teaspoon ground *emma* (Sichuan pepper)
10 mint leaves
1 tablespoon soy sauce
¼ teaspoon salt

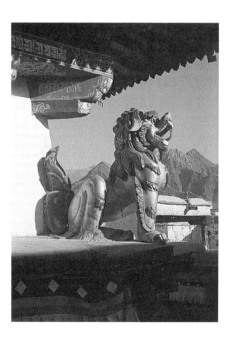

Chop the celery, cabbage, spinach, and green onion finely. It is important to chop the vegetables by hand; a food processor will make them mushy and the juices will be lost in the cooking. Sauté the onion in oil till brown and then add the garlic, ginger, paprika, *emma*, and mint. Cook the spices briefly, then remove from the heat and add the soy sauce and salt. Add the cooked mixture to the raw chopped vegetables. Toss lightly with the hands to mix all together.

Fill the *momos* and steam for 5–7 minutes.

Spinach Momo Filling 🍃

Tsoma Momo

Tsoma refers to any edible wild greens; you can use Swiss chard, mustard greens or other greens in combination with, or instead of, spinach. A favorite pastime for the Tibetan children at the farming settlements in south India is to go foraging together in the fields for wild greens. The kids enjoy the chance to be off on their own, and the grownups are happy because the children are being productive.

This recipe originally came from Tsering's mother, who also adds chilies to the mix. Tsering prefers to make the *momos* mild and serve them with chili sauce.

INGREDIENTS:

2 lbs. spinach
¼ cup oil
1½ onions, chopped
¾ teaspoon ground *emma* (Sichuan pepper)
3 cloves garlic, finely chopped
2 inches fresh ginger, finely chopped
6 green onions, chopped

Blanche the spinach in boiling water. Rinse it under cold water and drain, squeezing out as much moisture as possible. Chop the drained spinach finely.

Heat the oil over high heat. Add the onion and fry till it begins to brown. Add the garlic, ginger, and *emma* and fry briefly. Remove from the heat and stir in the green onions and spinach.

Fill the *momos*. Steam for 4 minutes only, as the filling is precooked.

Spinach and Cheese Momo Filling 🍒

Tse tang Chura Momo

Fresh *Chuship*, page 116, is ideal for this, and you can make the cheese on the same day, without leaving it to dry. Otherwise, you can use crumbled feta cheese, grated mozzarella, or ricotta blended with a little grated parmesan.

INGREDIENTS:

1 lb. spinach
1/4 cup oil
1 1/2 onions, chopped
3/4 teaspoon ground *emma* (Sichuan pepper)
3 cloves garlic, finely chopped
2 inches fresh ginger, finely chopped
6 green onions, chopped
1 lb. cheese

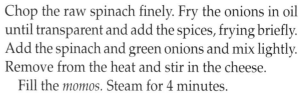

Chop the raw spinach finely. Fry the onions in oil until transparent and add the spices, frying briefly. Add the spinach and green onions and mix lightly. Remove from the heat and stir in the cheese.

Fill the *momos*. Steam for 4 minutes.

Beef Pastries

Sha Paley

These meat-filled, lightly fried pastries are a favorite food for picnics, because they keep well and pack easily. But they are at their very best when eaten hot out of the pan, and you will often find them served in Tibetan homes for almost any occasion. They have been called "Tibetan hamburgers" but really have more in common with empanadas, knishes, or Cornish pasties.

This recipe uses the same ingredients as *Sha Momo*, page 40, both for the dough and the beef filling. But the shape of the pastries and the method of cooking is completely different.

This recipe makes enough for eight pastries, which will feed four people as a main course, or double that number as an appetizer. However, it does provoke people to eat especially shamelessly.

PASTRY INGREDIENTS:

2½ cups flour
¾ cup water

Mix the flour and water into dough. The amount of water needed may vary slightly depending on the age of the flour. The dough should be as moist as for ordinary bread. Cover the dough and set it aside to rest while preparing the filling.

FILLING INGREDIENTS:

1 lb. ground beef
2 inches fresh ginger, finely chopped
4 cloves garlic, finely chopped
½ teaspoon ground *emma* (Sichuan pepper)
1 large onion, finely chopped
⅓ cup chopped green onion or chives
3 stalks celery, finely chopped
¼ teaspoon salt

Cook the ground beef with the garlic, ginger, and *emma* in a frying pan over medium heat, browning the meat well. Add the meat to the other filling ingredients and toss to mix thoroughly.

Tear the dough into lumps about 1½ inches in diameter. On a floured board, roll them out into circles about 4 inches across. Spread 2 tablespoons of filling in an even layer on one of the circles, leaving a narrow border of dough. Lay a second circle of dough on top.

Holding the sandwich in the palm of one hand, pinch the edge of the dough between your thumb and forefinger, and then use your thumb to fold the resulting flap onto itself. As you do so, pinch the edge again and repeat, moving slightly each time so that a continuous spiral seals the edges of the dough all round.

Some people use a shortcut to form the pastries, using a single circle of dough for each. They are shaped just like round *momos*, but extra-large, and then flattened by pressing between the palms. The resulting shapes are not nearly as pretty as the traditional ones.

Sha Paleh are usually deep fried, but we prefer to shallow fry them over medium heat with 1–2 tablespoons of oil. Turn them over once so that each side is golden brown.

Serve with any chili sauce.

Vegetable Pastries 🍏

Tse Paley

For a vegetarian version of *Sha Paley,* use the recipe for *Tse Momo*, page 42, to make the filling. Make the dough, fill it, shape it, and fry it exactly as for *Sha Paley.*

Noodle Dishes (Tukpa)

Although *tuk* usually refers to noodles, it can also mean any grain that is boiled in liquid, including porridge-like dishes made from *tsampa*, rice, or cracked wheat.

These meals-in-a-dish, high in carbohydrates, are eaten almost daily at the evening meal or, as leftovers, for breakfast. Tibetans avoid such food at lunchtime because it leaves you sleepy all afternoon. The porridge-like *tukpa* dishes are often fed to women after childbirth to help them regain strength.

The same basic broth is used in most of the *tukpa* recipes, and we have provided a vegetarian version as well.

> *Food tastes better when Mother serves it;*
> *Stories sound better when Father tells them.*
> —Tibetan proverb

Basic Tukpa Broth

If the recipe in which the broth is used calls for additional meat, make the broth with bones only. Otherwise, use bones with a fair amount of meat on them, such as oxtail.

INGREDIENTS:

1 lb. oxtail or other beef on the bone, or 1 lb. beef bones
1/4 teaspoon whole *emma* (Sichuan pepper)
5–6 cloves garlic
2 inches fresh ginger, crushed
3 quarts water
1/2 teaspoon salt

Boil the meat and spices together for at least one hour, until the meat is very soft. Remove the bones. Cool the broth and remove any fat from the surface.

Vegetable Tukpa Broth

This makes a very light, clean-tasting vegetable broth. Feel free to use any vegetarian stock in place of the water in this recipe. If you like, save potato peelings for a vegetable stock pot or use vegetarian bouillon or Vegex.

INGREDIENTS:

1 tablespoon vegetable oil
1 onion, coarsely chopped
1 inch fresh ginger, chopped
3 cloves garlic, chopped
2 tomatoes, coarsely chopped
9 cups water

In a large pot, sauté the onion, ginger, and garlic in oil until browned. Add the tomato and water, and bring to a boil. Simmer for 15 minutes.

Pulled Noodles in Beef Soup

Tentuk

Tentuk is a favorite throughout Tibet, a hearty meal-in-a-dish that takes little effort. The name means "pulled noodles," referring to the simple technique of tearing off small, roughly shaped, flat pieces of dough. This particular version of *tentuk* comes from the eastern region of Amdo.

NOODLE INGREDIENTS:

2 cups flour
2/3 cup water

Mix the flour and water into a dough, kneading it until very elastic. Roll the dough into a cylinder the thickness of a finger. Brush it with oil, cover it, and let it sit while you prepare the remaining ingredients.

SOUP INGREDIENTS:

1 tablespoon oil
1/2 onion, chopped
1 clove garlic, chopped
1 teaspoon fresh ginger, chopped
1 lb. top round beef, thinly sliced
1 tomato, chopped
4-inch piece daikon, thinly sliced
Basic *Tukpa* Broth, page 48
leaves of 1 daikon, or 1/2 bunch spinach, chopped
salt

Sauté the onion, garlic, and ginger in a deep pot until the onion begins to brown. Add the beef and stir-fry till cooked. Add the tomato, daikon, and the prepared broth. Bring to a full boil.

Prepare the greens and have them ready at hand, but do not add them to the soup yet. Flatten the dough cylinder by pinching it into long strips between your thumb and fingers. Then pull small pieces off the ribbons of dough, tossing them directly into the boiling broth.

When all the noodles have been added, turn off the heat and stir in the chopped greens. Add salt to taste.

Pulled Noodles in Vegetable Soup 🍒

Tse Tentuk

This is a vegetarian version of the traditional *tentuk*, the hearty noodle soup popular throughout Tibet. Feel free to improvise and add other vegetables in season. As it stands, this version is simple and light, with the last-minute addition of tomato and green onions providing a remarkably fresh flavor.

NOODLE INGREDIENTS:

2 cups flour
⅔ cup water

Mix the flour and water into a dough, kneading it until very elastic. Roll the dough into a cylinder the thickness of a finger. Brush it with oil, cover it, and let it sit while you prepare the remaining ingredients.

SOUP INGREDIENTS:

1 tomato
2 green onions
leaves of 1 daikon, or ½ bunch spinach
Vegetable *Tukpa* Broth, page 48
4-inch piece daikon, thinly sliced
salt

Chop the tomato and the green onions very finely, as if making a salsa. Chop the spinach or daikon greens coarsely and set them aside. Bring the broth to a full boil in a large pot, and add the sliced daikon.

Flatten the dough cylinder by pinching it into long strips between your thumb and fingers. Then pull small pieces off the ribbons of dough, tossing them directly into the boiling broth. When all the noodles have been added, turn off the heat and stir in the chopped greens. Add salt to taste. Add the chopped tomato and green onion at the very last moment before serving.

Egg Noodles in Beef Soup

Gutse Rituk

Gutse Rituk is identical to *Tentuk*, page 49, except that it is made with richer, firmer egg noodles.

NOODLE INGREDIENTS:

2 cups flour
2 eggs
1/3 cup water

SOUP INGREDIENTS:

1 tablespoon oil
1/2 onion, chopped
1 clove garlic, chopped
1 teaspoon fresh ginger, chopped
1 lb. top round beef, thinly sliced
1 tomato, chopped
4-inch piece daikon, thinly sliced
Basic *Tukpa* Broth, page 48
leaves of 1 daikon or 1/2 bunch spinach, chopped
salt

Mix the flour and eggs together, and add water to make a stiff dough, kneading it until very elastic. (The amount of water needed may vary.) Cover the dough and let it rest for half an hour.

Sauté the onion, garlic, and ginger in oil in a deep pot until the onion begins to brown. Add the beef and stir-fry. When fully cooked, add the tomato and dai-kon, along with the prepared broth. Bring to the boil.

On a floured surface, roll or pat the dough into a round three quarters of an inch thick and cut it into thin strips with a sharp knife. Roll each strip between two hands till it is as thin as your little finger. Tear the strips into half-inch pieces. Rub each piece in a curling motion with your thumb against the palm of the other hand to make small hollow shell shapes. Sprinkle the noodle shapes with flour to keep them from sticking together.

Add the noodles to the boiling broth all at once. Boil for 2–3 minutes. Turn off the heat and stir in the chopped greens. Add salt to taste.

Egg Noodles in Vegetable Soup 🌶

Tse Gutse Rituk

This is a meatless adaptation of the traditional *Gutse Rituk*, page 51.

NOODLE INGREDIENTS:
2 cups flour
2 eggs
1/3 cup water

SOUP INGREDIENTS:
1 tablespoon oil
1/2 onion, chopped
1 clove garlic, chopped
1 teaspoon fresh ginger, chopped
1 tomato, chopped
4-inch piece daikon, thinly sliced
Vegetable *Tukpa* Broth, page 48
leaves of 1 daikon or 1/2 bunch spinach, chopped
salt

Mix the flour and eggs together, and add water to make a stiff dough, kneading it until very elastic. (The amount of water needed may vary.) Cover the dough and let it rest for half an hour.

Sauté the onion, garlic, and ginger in oil in a deep pot until the onion begins to brown. Add the tomato and daikon slices, along with the prepared broth. Bring to the boil.

On a floured surface, roll or pat the dough into a round three-quarters of an inch thick and cut it into thin strips with a sharp knife. Roll each strip between two hands till it is as thin as your little finger. Tear the strips into half-inch pieces. Rub each piece in a curling motion with your thumb against the palm of the other hand to make small hollow shell shapes. Sprinkle the noodle shapes with flour to keep them from sticking together.

Add the noodles to the boiling broth all at once. Boil for 2–3 minutes. Turn off the heat and stir in the chopped greens. Add salt to taste.

Momo Soup

Motuk

Motuk is really just a dish of *momos* served in a light broth, rather like wonton soup. When *momos* are made for soup, they are usually slightly smaller than usual, with a characteristic elongated shape. Of course, you can use *momos* of any shape or size you like. If you happen to have some frozen *momos* on hand, these also work well in *Motuk.*

This is a traditional version made with beef *momos,* but it would also be very good made with chicken *momos* cooked in chicken broth.

INGREDIENTS:

Basic *Tukpa* Broth, page 48
Basic *Momo* Dough, page 37
Beef *Momo* Filling, page 40
½ bunch spinach, or Swiss chard

Make the *momo* dough and filling. To make the special shape for *Motuk,* hold a circle of dough in your left hand and place a tablespoon of filling in the center. Use your thumb and forefinger to pinch a small fold in the edge of the circle. Continue pinching the two edges together, alternating the pressure from side to side, first pressing thumb to forefinger, then forefinger to thumb. With your other thumb, keep pushing the filling in towards the center. Finish with a pinch at the end to make a tail.

If you are using Swiss chard, remove the ribs and stems first. Chop the greens. Bring the broth to a boil over high heat. Add the *momos* all at once. When the broth returns to a boil, turn the heat down and simmer for 7–10 minutes, or until the *momos* rise to the surface. Remove from the heat and stir in the chopped greens.

Serve with any chili sauce.

Vegetable Momo Soup 🐦

Motuk Tse

This is a meatless version of the traditional *Motuk*, with tofu and bean thread noodles added to make a more substantial meal. See the previous recipe for *Motuk* for instructions on making the special *momo* shapes used in soup. Or, you can use *momos* of any shape or size, including frozen ones if you have some already made.

INGREDIENTS:

1 bunch (2 oz.) bean thread noodles
Basic *Momo* Dough, page 37
Vegetable *Momo* Filling, page 42, or Spinach *Momo* Filling, page 43, or Spinach and Cheese *Momo* Filling, page 44
½ bunch spinach, or Swiss chard
Vegetable *Tukpa* Broth, page 48
1 cake (12 oz.) tofu, cut into ½-inch cubes
¼ lb. mushrooms, thinly sliced
½ cup green peas

Soak the bean thread noodles in enough hot water to cover them as they swell, for 20–30 minutes. Make the *momo* dough and filling, and shape the *momos*.

Drain the noodles and cut them into short lengths. If you are using Swiss chard, remove the ribs and stems first. Chop the greens and set aside.

Add the tofu and mushrooms to the broth and boil for 1–2 minutes. Add the vegetable *momos* to the broth all at once. When the *momos* start to rise to the surface, add the noodles and peas. As soon as the broth begins to boil again, remove from the heat and stir in the greens.

Serve with any chili sauce.

Holiday Dumpling Soup 🍃

Peeshi

This is similar to *Motuk*, except that *Peeshi* are dumplings shaped more like wontons. This is party food, because shaping the stuffed dough packets takes a lot of time. On holidays at the farming settlement, the women chat and make *peeshi* while the men gamble. For a vegetarian *peeshi*, simply use the vegetarian versions of the *tukpa* broth and *momo* filling.

INGREDIENTS:

Basic *Tukpa* Broth, page 48, or Vegetable *Tukpa* Broth, page 48

Basic *Momo* Dough, page 37

Beef *Momo* Filling, page 40, or any vegetarian *momo* filling, pages 42-44

Prepare the *momo* dough and filling. Roll the dough out to a large flat sheet and cut it into triangles. Traditionally this is done by loosely rolling up the sheet of dough and cutting the roll into 2-inch wide strips. The strips are then unrolled and cut diagonally into triangles.

(1) Place 1 teaspoon of filling at the corner of each triangle. (2) Roll up the filled corner toward the opposite side of the triangle. (3) Pinch the two ends of the roll together, overlapping.

Bring the broth to a boil over high heat. Add the dumplings all at once. When the broth returns to a boil, turn the heat down and simmer for 7–10 minutes, or until the dumplings rise to the surface.

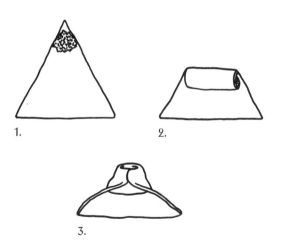

1.

2.

3.

Flat Noodles in Beef Soup

Tukpa Chitsi

Chitsi are flat wheat noodles, very similar to Italian fettuccine.

INGREDIENTS:

1 tablespoon oil
½ onion, chopped
1 clove garlic
1 teaspoon fresh ginger, chopped
1 lb. top round beef, thinly sliced
1 tomato, chopped
Basic *Tukpa* Broth, page 48
1 lb. fresh fettuccine, or ½ lb. dry pasta

In a large pot, sauté the onion till brown. Add the garlic and ginger. Add the beef and stir till cooked. Add the tomato and broth and bring to the boil. Add the pasta to the boiling broth and cook until it is tender.

Flat Noodles in Vegetable Broth 🍃

Tse Chitsi Tukpa

This is a vegetarian adaptation of the traditional *Tukpa Chitsi*.

INGREDIENTS:

1 tablespoon oil
½ onion, chopped
1 clove garlic
1 teaspoon fresh ginger, chopped
1 tomato, chopped
Vegetable *Tukpa* Broth, page 48
1 lb. fresh fettuccine,
    or ½ lb. dry pasta

In a large pot, sauté the onion till brown. Add the garlic and ginger. Add the tomato and broth and bring to the boil. Add the pasta to the boiling broth and cook until it is tender.

Fried Noodles 🍃

Tukpa Ngopa

In Lhasa this dish is called *ta ja,* which means "fried flat." The crispy cake of fried noodles topped with a savory stir-fry is very popular at the restaurant, especially among vegetarians.

The very fine noodles are difficult to make by hand, so we recommend using fresh angel hair pasta or very finely cut fresh Chinese egg noodles. In Tibet, or at the settlements in India, a neighbor who is known for his skill at cutting noodles would be asked to lend a hand. Such an expert might well be an ex-monk; one can gain a lot of experience producing the huge volume of noodles required for monastery meals.

For a vegetarian version, simply omit the meat. You can add other vegetables if you like. Snow peas, mushrooms, cauliflower, and broccoli are all good, and the dish lends itself to improvisation.

INGREDIENTS:

1 lb. fresh angel hair pasta, or fresh thin-cut
    egg noodles
oil for frying
1 onion, chopped
3 cloves garlic, finely chopped
2 inches fresh ginger, finely chopped
1 lb. top round beef, thinly sliced [optional]
2 stalks celery, sliced thin on diagonal
1 carrot, sliced thin on diagonal
4 baby bok choy or 1/4 head cabbage, sliced thinly

In a large pot of salted water, boil the noodles until just cooked. Drain and toss them with a little oil so they do not stick. Spread them to cool on a tray or cookie sheet.

Heat a lightly oiled, nonstick frying pan. When hot, spread one fourth of the noodles evenly in the frying pan. They should be flat, not heaped. Fry till crisp and brown underneath, then flip to fry the other side. Repeat to make four crispy noodle cakes and place on individual plates.

Fry the onion, garlic, and ginger till brown. Add the meat and stir-fry one minute. Add the remaining vegetables and stir-fry for two more minutes, or until barely cooked but still crisp. Spread the stir-fried mixture on top of the noodle cakes in four equal portions.

Cracked Wheat Porridge

Drotuk

Drotuk is served for breakfast or dinner, and as an auspicious dish at Losar, the new year celebration. It is not much liked by younger Tibetans who grew up in the refugee settlements. They call it ugly and boring, having eaten too many meals of the cracked wheat, often worm-eaten, that came in foreign aid shipments.

If you do not have any of the slightly sweet and very hard dried cheese called *churkam*, simply omit it as there is no good substitute.

INGREDIENTS:

1 cup cracked wheat
1 lb. beef bones
½ lb. minced beef
8 cups water
½ cup *Churkam*, page 117

Wash the cracked wheat and add it to the beef bones, beef, and water in a large pot. Boil until the wheat is the consistency of a thin porridge, at least 1 hour, stirring occasionally. You may need to add extra water. *Drotuk* should be thin enough to pour like a liquid. Add the cheese and cook for 20 minutes more, or until the cheese is soft enough to be chewable.

Rice Porridge

Dretuk

This is similar to *Drotuk*, page 58, but made with rice instead of wheat, and the dried *churkam* cheese is optional here as well. Tsering's mother churns her *dretuk* in a butter churn to make it very smooth. A blender works just as well.

Wash the rice and add it to the beef bones and water in a large pot. Boil until the mixture is the consistency of a thin porridge, about 1 hour. It should be thin enough to pour like a liquid. You may need to add extra water. You can run it through a blender in several batches, which will shorten the cooking time needed to reach the right consistency.

Add the cheese and cook for 20 minutes more.

Serve with any chili sauce.

INGREDIENTS:

1 cup rice
1 lb. beef bones
½ lb. minced beef (optional)
8 cups water
½ cup *Churkam*, page 117

Barley Porridge

Tsampa Tukpa (Tsamtuk)

Tsampa tukpa is often fed to mothers recovering from childbirth. The meaty barley porridge is restorative, both hearty and easy to digest.

INGREDIENTS:
Basic *Tukpa* Broth, page 48
½ lb. beef
1½ cups *Tsampa*, page 95

Chop the beef very finely by hand or in a food processor. Bring the broth to a boil and stir in the chopped beef. Mix the *tsampa* flour with a little water to make paste that is thin enough to pour. Stir the *tsampa* paste into the boiling broth. Serve immediately while still very hot. The soup will thicken considerably if left to cool.

MEAT DISHES (SHA)

In spite of their profound belief in the sanctity of all life and desire to avoid killing animals, most Tibetans genuinely enjoy eating meat. The ambivalence results from a climate that favors herding over the cultivation of plant crops, and centuries of nomadic culture dependent on meat and dairy products. Not only do Tibetans have a huge appetite for meat by present Western standards, they also relish the fat, bones, skin, and organ meats that Westerners now avoid.

Yak and mutton are the meats most often eaten in Tibet, and goat is quite common. Pork and beef are also eaten, but more rarely. Most people avoid chicken and fish: the smaller the animal, the more lives that must be taken to feed a given number of people. However, the rules are not rigid, and families that keep chickens for eggs or who live near a bountiful stream will occasionally indulge. Buffalo is forbidden because the animal has a special relationship with certain deities.

At Lhasa Moon, Tsering uses top round beef for most dishes that would call for yak. A more traditional approach would use fattier cuts of beef, usually on the bone. Even in dishes that include a lot sauce or meat cut into small pieces, Tibetans would prefer to nibble at the bones. It draws out the meal, allowing more time for conversation and socializing.

You will also find several meat dishes included under *Snacks and Appetizers*, pages 28-36.

Beef Stew with Bean Thread Noodles

Ping Sha

Ping sha makes an appearance at most festive meals, including weddings and Losar celebrations. The dish is auspicious because the long noodles represent long life. The best *ping* noodles, available in Asian markets, are made from mung beans, but green bean noodles (*sai fun*) are also good. Don't use rice noodles as they are too mushy. Italian vermicelli works reasonably well; boil it as you normally would rather than soaking it like bean thread noodles.

In Tibet this dish is usually made with ribs cut into short pieces, but we prefer a boneless cut of beef.

INGREDIENTS:

1 bunch bean thread noodles (2 oz.)

3 waxy potatoes

1 tablespoon oil

1 small onion, coarsely chopped

1 teaspoon paprika

2 cloves garlic, chopped

1 inch fresh ginger, chopped

¼ teaspoon crushed *emma* (Sichuan pepper)

1 tomato, coarsely chopped

1 lb. top round beef, cut into 1-inch cubes

½ cup peas

salt to taste

Cover the noodles in hot water, with room to expand, and leave them to soak for 20 minutes.

Boil the potatoes till just tender but not soft. Peel them and cut them into bite-size chunks.

In a large pot, sauté the onion in oil with the paprika until translucent. Add the garlic, ginger, and *emma,* and cook another minute. Add the meat and stir-fry until browned. Add the tomato and enough water to cover. Turn the heat up high until it begins to boil, then lower the heat and simmer for half an hour. Add the peas and potatoes and one more cup of water.

Drain the bean threads and cut them with scissors a few times to make them easier to serve. Stir the bean threads into the stew and heat through. Add salt to taste.

Mushrooms with Beef and Mixed Vegetables

Sesha

This is a modern adaptation that Tsering has created for Lhasa Moon. The original dish involves roasting the mushrooms over an open fire, then chopping and frying them with onion and crushed chilies, and cooking them into a porridgy mush thickened with *tsampa*. Tsering's version is equally tasty and much more visually appealing. The broccoli, which is unknown in Tibet, is also a new addition that adds freshness and color.

INGREDIENTS:

1 lb. mushrooms
1 large carrot
2 tablespoons oil
2 cloves of garlic, crushed
$1/8$ teaspoon ground black pepper
salt to taste

1 clove garlic, chopped
1 lb. broccoli, cut into florets
$1/2$ red pepper, cut into 1-inch pieces
1 lb. top round beef

Cut the mushrooms in half if small, or slice them in thirds if they are larger. Don't slice them too thin or they will get mushy. Cut the carrot into 1-inch lengths and then cut them vertically into square slices about $1/4$ inch thick. Cut up the remaining vegetables. Cut the beef into thin slices $1/8$ inch thick and about 2 inches square.

In a wide, flat pan, fry the mushrooms over high heat with the garlic, black pepper, and salt, until they just begin to brown.

Coat a second pan with a little oil, and heat till very hot. Spread the meat evenly in the pan in a single layer and cook for one or two minutes without stirring. Turn the pieces over and cook for another minute. Add the carrots, broccoli, and red pepper and stir-fry for one more minute. Cover the pan and let it steam for another minute. Stir in the mushrooms and serve.

Lamb Curry

Luksha Shamdeh

This lamb curry is typical of the dishes introduced to Tibet by Tibetan Muslims who traveled as traders to India long before the Tibetans came to India as refugees. It is milder than most Indian curries, and equally good served with rice or bread.

The yogurt acts as a tenderizer on the meat, as well as adding a distinctive flavor.

MARINADE INGREDIENTS:

1 cup plain yogurt
1 tablespoon paprika
1 teaspoon curry powder
1 tablespoon soy sauce
1 teaspoon garlic, finely chopped
1 teaspoon fresh ginger, finely chopped

MAIN INGREDIENTS:

1 lb. boned leg of lamb, cut into 2-inch cubes
1 tablespoon oil
3 large onions
1 cinnamon stick
1 star anise
5 cloves
2–3 bay leaves
4 tomatoes, quartered
3 potatoes

Mix together the yogurt, paprika, curry powder, soy sauce, garlic, and ginger. Add the lamb, mixing well to coat each piece, and let it marinate overnight or at least for a few hours.

Cut the onions coarsely into chunks and sauté them in the oil till translucent. Add the cinnamon stick, star anise, cloves, and bay leaves and continue cooking until the onion browns and begins to dry out. Add the meat, along with the marinade, to the onions. When the mixture begins to boil, add the tomatoes.

Boil the curry over medium heat for 20 minutes. Then turn the heat to low, cover the pot and simmer slowly for 40 minutes more. Boil the potatoes separately till just cooked. Cut them into quarters and stir them into the curry five minutes before finishing.

Chicken Curry

Chasha Shamdeh

This is another curry that Tibetan Muslim traders brought home from India. Like *Luksha Shamdeh,* the yogurt marinade tenderizes the meat as well as creating a sauce.

The typical *garam masala* used in Tibetan cooking is a mixture of coriander, cardamom, cinnamon, and bay leaf (page 18).

MARINADE INGREDIENTS:

2 cups plain yogurt
3 cloves garlic, chopped
1/3 cup soy sauce
1 tablespoon paprika

MAIN INGREDIENTS:

2 lbs. chicken pieces on the bone
3 onions, chopped
1/4 cup oil
1 teaspoon curry powder
3/4 teaspoon whole cloves
4 cloves garlic, chopped
1 tablespoon paprika
1 teaspoon *garam masala*
2 cinnamon sticks
3 tomatoes, chopped
1/2 teaspoon salt

Mix together the marinade of yogurt, garlic, soy sauce, and paprika. Mix in the chicken pieces and leave for at least half an hour, ideally for several hours or overnight.

Fry the onions in oil over high heat till translucent. Add the remaining spices and continue cooking till the onions are very soft and starting to dry out. Add the tomatoes and salt, stirring till the tomatoes give off their juices and start to cook dry. Add the chicken with the marinade. Stir occasionally over high heat until it just begins to boil, then simmer for about 40 minutes over very low heat.

Lamb with Daikon

Labu Dikrul

Mutton stewed with daikon is a very popular dish in the countryside and amongst nomads, eaten all over Tibet with slightly different methods of cooking in each region. Tibetans consider it an especially appropriate dish to carry on a pilgrimage or other journey. It is excellent when made in advance and the flavors allowed to meld.

This particular version originates in Kham and would be prepared for a special treat at home rather than a meal on the road. It includes a few extra steps, in which the meat and vegetables are fried after stewing and the sauce is reduced. You can make the simpler dish (called *Sha Dotzu*) that is familiar throughout Tibet by omitting these last steps. *Labu Dikrul* is best served with the steamed rolls called *Tingmo* (page 92) to soak up the juices, but is also very good with rice.

INGREDIENTS:

1 lb. (boneless weight) lamb shank

2 lbs. daikon

2 large onions

3 inches fresh ginger

1/4 teaspoon ground *emma* (Sichuan pepper)

5 cloves garlic

salt

1 tablespoon oil

1/2 teaspoon paprika

1 medium tomato, chopped

daikon leaves or spinach (1/2 to 1 bunch, depending on taste)

Place the lamb (with bones if available) in a large pot. Add the daikon cut into 2-inch slices and one of the onions, cut into quarters. Crush the ginger coarsely with the flat of a knife, leaving the skin on, and add it to the pot with the whole cloves of garlic and the ground *emma*. Add enough cold water to cover, and bring to a boil. Turn the heat down and simmer for 1 1/2 hours, until all the fat from the meat is absorbed into the daikon, which turns translucent. Add salt to taste. Remove the lamb and daikon from the liquid. At this point the simpler version of the dish is ready to serve, and the broth would be saved for another purpose.

Cut the lamb and daikon into 1-inch cubes, and chop the tomato. Chop the second onion very finely. In a large pot fry the onion in oil over high heat till brown. Add the paprika, and fry briefly till the color changes. Add the tomato, lamb, daikon, and enough of the broth to just cover the meat and vegetables. Stir over a very hot fire, boiling rapidly to reduce the broth slightly. Chop the daikon leaves or spinach. Place the greens on top of the meat without stirring and cover tightly to steam for one minute. Stir the greens into the stew just before serving.

Himalayan Chicken

Chasha Himalaya

This is an invention of Tsering's. The chicken is fried crisp like *Chasha Katsa* (page 35), and then a tangy sauce is added. Use thigh and leg meat; breast will dry out when fried in this way. Serve this dish with rice.

MARINADE INGREDIENTS:

1/4 cup soy sauce
1/4 teaspoon garlic, finely chopped
1/4 teaspoon fresh ginger, finely chopped
1 teaspoon paprika
1/4 teaspoon ground *emma* (Sichuan pepper)

MAIN INGREDIENTS:

1 lb. boned chicken
oil for deep frying
2 onions, chopped
1/4 teaspoon paprika
1/4 teaspoon fresh ginger, chopped
1/4 teaspoon garlic, chopped
1/2 teaspoon salt
3 tomatoes, chopped
2 jalapeño chilies, chopped (optional)

Cut the chicken into bite-sized cubes. Mix the soy sauce and spices for the marinade. Add the chicken and mix by hand to coat each piece. Let the mixture sit for at least half an hour, and preferably overnight.

Pour vegetable oil in a pan to a depth of $1\frac{1}{2}$ inches, and heat thoroughly. Using chop sticks or tongs, take the meat directly from the marinade a few pieces at a time and fry in the oil. It will splatter fiercely. Be careful not to crowd the pieces. Turn them over to cook both sides until brown, about 2–3 minutes. Drain on paper towels.

Fry the onions in a tablespoon of oil with the paprika, ginger, garlic, and salt, until the onions brown. Stir in the tomatoes and chilies, and cook till the tomatoes form a sauce.

Add the fried chicken to the sauce just before serving, and stir in lightly.

Potatoes with Stir-fried Beef

Shogo Ngopa

Use the waxy type of potatoes for this dish. Baking potatoes will fall apart.

INGREDIENTS:

1 lb. top round beef
6 medium-small potatoes
1 tablespoon oil
$\frac{1}{2}$ onion, coarsely chopped
2 cloves garlic, finely chopped
$\frac{1}{2}$ tomato, finely chopped
$\frac{1}{4}$ cup fresh or frozen peas
1 tablespoon cilantro leaves, finely chopped

Cut the beef into thin slices, $\frac{1}{4}$ inch thick and about $1\frac{1}{2}$–2 inches square. Boil the potatoes till just tender. Drain them and cut them in half lengthwise. Then slice them into half circles about $\frac{1}{3}$ inch thick.

Sauté the onion till translucent. Add the meat and stir-fry till just cooked. Add the peas, tomato, and potatoes and stir-fry for one minute. Add 1 cup of warm water and heat through. Sprinkle the chopped cilantro on top just before serving.

Browned Beef with Vegetables

Shaptak

Shaptak literally means "burnt meat" and sometimes refers to barbecue, but it is also the name for this fried meat dish that is eaten all over Tibet in slightly different versions. It is good served with a bread such as *Paley*, page 90.

INGREDIENTS:

1 lb. top round beef
2 tablespoons oil
1 large red onion, chopped coarsely
½ teaspoon paprika
2 cloves garlic, chopped
1 inch fresh ginger, chopped
¼ teaspoon ground *emma* (Sichuan pepper)
1 tomato, chopped coarsely
½ green bell pepper
½ red bell pepper

Cut the beef into thin slices about ⅛ inch thick and 1½ to 2 inches square. Cut the red and green bell peppers into very thin slices.

Heat a frying pan very hot with 1 tablespoon of the oil. Spread the beef slices out in a single layer in the pan, and fry till just cooked. Repeat in batches until all the beef is cooked.

In a separate pan, sauté the onion in a little oil with the paprika, garlic, ginger, and *emma*, until the onion turns translucent. Add the tomato and cook till soft. Stir in the bell peppers and beef.

Kongpo-style Browned Beef

Kongpo Shaptak

Tsering's mother provided this recipe. The combination of pungent cheese and hot chilies is characteristic of many dishes from Kongpo, where her family originated. It is very good with a bread such as *Paley*, page 90, or *Tingmo*, page 92.

INGREDIENTS:

1 lb. top round beef
2 tablespoons oil
1 large red onion, chopped coarsely
½ teaspoon paprika
2 cloves garlic, chopped
1 inch fresh ginger, chopped
¼ teaspoon ground *emma* (Sichuan pepper)
1 tomato, chopped coarsely
1½ tablespoons *Churu*, page 118, or blue cheese, crumbled
1 cup water
2 jalapeño chilies, sliced thinly on diagonal

Cut the beef into thin slices about ⅛ inch thick and 1½ to 2 inches square.

Heat the pan over high heat, and add the oil. Fry the onion till brown, with the paprika, garlic, ginger, and *emma*. Add the beef and stir-fry till cooked through. Add the tomato and the cheese and cook till the cheese melts. Add the water and stir in the chilies, cooking for a few minutes more.

Boiled Pork

Paksha Tsoba

Boiled pork is popular amongst Tibetans, prepared very simply and served with hot sauce. The fat and skin are considered a delicacy, and a little of each should be included on each slice of meat.

INGREDIENTS:

1 lb. (boneless weight) pork belly, with skin

Cut the meat into 3 or 4 large pieces, with some skin on each. Place the meat in a pot and cover with cold water. Bring to a boil, and simmer for 45–60 minutes. Drain the pork and slice it thinly.

Serve with any chili sauce.

Pork with Daikon

Paksha Labu

This is similar to *Labu Dikrul*, using pork instead of lamb. The daikon absorbs the flavors of the meat and balances its richness. Tibetans prefer the skin and fat left on the pork. You can remove it if you like. The dish is equally good served hot or cold.

INGREDIENTS:

1 lb. (boneless weight) pork belly, with skin
2 lbs. daikon
2 large onions
3 inches fresh ginger
¼ teaspoon ground *emma* (Sichuan pepper)
5 cloves garlic
salt
½ teaspoon paprika
1 medium tomato, chopped

Place the pork (with the bones if possible) in a large pot. Add the daikon, cut into 2-inch chunks, and one of the onions, cut into quarters. Crush the ginger coarsely with the flat of a knife, leaving the skin on, and add it to the pot with the whole cloves of garlic and the ground *emma*. Add enough cold water to cover, and bring to a boil. Turn the heat down and simmer for 1½ hours. Add salt to taste.

Remove the pork and daikon from the liquid. Cut the daikon and the pork into thin slices, including a little fat and skin on each slice of meat. Lay the slices out on a plate, alternating the pork and daikon.

Serve with Coriander Chili Sauce (*Sonam Penzom Sibeh*), page 121.

String Beans with Beef

Tema tang Sha

When cooking for a large family or unexpected guests, Tibetans will often add potatoes to stretch this dish. We have included potatoes only in the vegetarian version, *Tema*, page 80.

Marinating the meat for extra flavor is optional. It is Tsering's own addition, as marinades are not normally used in Tibetan cooking.

Cut the meat into thin strips about the size and shape of French fries. You can marinate the meat for half an hour in soy sauce mixed with a little chopped garlic, paprika, and ground *emma*. Cut the string beans diagonally into 1½-inch pieces. Slice the red pepper very thinly.

Fry the onion in oil over high heat until softened, along with the additional garlic, paprika, and ginger. Add the meat and stir-fry until just cooked rare. Stir in the chili and tomato, then add the string beans and stir-fry till just tender, about 8–9 minutes. Add the soy sauce, red pepper, and salt, stirring in quickly.

OPTIONAL MARINADE INGREDIENTS:

⅓ cup soy sauce
2 cloves garlic, finely chopped
½ teaspoon paprika
¼ teaspoon ground *emma* (Sichuan pepper)

MAIN INGREDIENTS:

1 lb. top round beef
1 lb. string beans
½ small red pepper
1 tablespoon oil
½ onion, chopped
2 cloves garlic, finely chopped
½ teaspoon paprika
1 inch fresh ginger, finely chopped
1 jalapeño chili, coarsely chopped
½ tomato, chopped
1 teaspoon soy sauce
salt to taste

Chayote with Beef

Iskus

Chayote is a pale green, oval vegetable with very firm flesh and a flavor similar to summer squash. You can find it in Asian and Mexican markets. Zucchini would make a reasonable substitute, but don't peel it, and cook it for slightly less time.

INGREDIENTS:

2 chayotes
1 lb. top round beef
1 tablespoon oil
½ onion, chopped
1 teaspoon paprika
2 cloves garlic, chopped
4 whole dry chilies
½ tomato, coarsely chopped
salt to taste

Peel the chayote and cut it in half lengthwise. Use a spoon to scoop out the seed, and cut the flesh into slices ⅛ inch thick. Wash the slices under running water to remove the sticky juice, and then drain them. Cut the beef into slices about ⅛ inch thick and 1½ to 2 inches square.

Fry the onion in oil over high heat, along with the paprika and garlic. When the onion is just beginning to brown, add the beef and stir-fry for one or two minutes. Add the chilies, being careful not to break them—you probably don't want the seeds to come out. Stir in the tomato, chayote, and salt. Cover and cook over medium heat 6–7 minutes.

Tibetan Hot Pot

Gyakor

This is a Tibetan version of a dish often known as Mongolian hot pot, which actually originated with the Moslem nomads of Mongolia and northern China. It is a special occasion dish, prepared only in the households of the aristocracy of central Tibet, a good indication of foreign origin. The name *gyakor* means "a hundred different ingredients."

The *gyakor* pot, available in Asian stores, has a central tube that holds charcoal, and an outer ring where the food cooks. It is sometimes a do-it-yourself affair: an array of meats and vegetables is served raw, to be dipped in the simmering broth at the table using chopsticks or a small strainer. Another way of presenting *gyakor* involves packing the meat and vegetables into the outer ring of the pot and then pouring boiling broth over them. The whole assembly cooks by the heat of the charcoal embers, and guests serve themselves from the pot. Either way, the broth can be served as a soup at the end of the meal. At least one chili sauce for dipping is essential. The steamed bread called *Tingmo*, page 92, is a good accompaniment.

Prepare the broth well in advance of the meal so you have time to cool it and remove the fat.

BROTH INGREDIENTS:

2–3 lbs. beef bones
3 inches fresh ginger, crushed
1 whole bulb garlic, unpeeled
1/4 teaspoon whole *emma* (Sichuan pepper)
1/2 teaspoon salt

Place the bones and seasonings in a deep pot and add water to about 2 inches above the bones. Boil for 1 1/2 hours. Let it cool and remove the fat.

Reheat the broth when you are ready to serve the *gyakor.* Put hot charcoal embers into the central tube of the *gyakor* pot, and then pour the hot broth into the outer ring of the pot.

Slice a selection of meats paper-thin and lay them out on a serving plate. For most recipes in this book, we have allowed 1/4 lb. meat per serving, but you will find that people often eat a lot more when it is presented this way. You can include any good cuts of beef or lamb, pork loin, or chicken breast.

Present a selection of vegetables, including any of the following:

MAIN INGREDIENTS:

spinach leaves
Swiss chard leaves, cut into 2-inch squares
carrots, thinly sliced in rectangles
celery, diagonally sliced
daikon, sliced in 1/8-inch rounds
snow peas
cabbage leaves, cut into 2-inch squares
potato, sliced in 1/8-inch rounds
mung bean noodles
wood ear fungus

Amounts will depend on the number of choices you offer. If you include mung bean noodles or wood ear fungus, each should be soaked in hot water separately for 20 minutes and then drained.

Cabbage Stir-fry

Logo Petse tang Sha

Logo Petse is usually made with pork or other red meat, but is also very good with chicken. The cabbage grown in Tibet is similar to our ordinary white or green round-headed cabbage, not the Chinese or Napa cabbage.

INGREDIENTS:

1 carrot
¼ head cabbage
1 lb. boneless chicken or pork loin
1 tablespoon oil
½ onion, chopped
1 teaspoon paprika
2 cloves garlic, finely chopped
2 jalapeño chilies, coarsely chopped
1 inch fresh ginger, finely chopped
1 red bell pepper, thinly sliced
salt to taste

Cut the carrot into 1½ inch lengths, and then lengthwise into rectangular slices about ⅛ inch thick. Cut the cabbage into 1-inch chunks. Cut the meat into 1-inch cubes or thin slices.

Sauté the onion in oil over high heat, along with the paprika, garlic, ginger, and jalapeños, until the onions begin to brown. Add the meat and stir-fry till cooked through. Add the carrots and stir-fry for one minute, then add the cabbage and stir-fry one more minute. Stir in the red bell pepper and salt to taste just before serving.

VEGETABLE DISHES (TSE)

Because much of Tibet's cold, high terrain supports little agriculture other than herding, a vegetarian diet is not a practical option for most of the population, in spite of their beliefs as Buddhists. For most Tibetans, vegetarianism has traditionally been an occasional ascetic practice, reserved for sacred days.

This picture is changing amongst Tibetans in exile. Vegetarianism is not only practical but very common in the surrounding Indian communities, and meat is an expensive luxury for most Tibetans living in the refugee settlements.

The standard Tibetan approach to cooking vegetables is to make a base of fried onion, garlic, ginger, and chopped tomato, with perhaps some soy sauce. Then add vegetables cut into uniform pieces, and stir-fry the mixture until the vegetables are tender. This is a reliable all-purpose method, but you will find a lot more variety in the recipes that follow. Many of the dishes included in this section are adaptations of traditional dishes that normally contain meat.

Throughout the book you will find other meatless dishes marked ❧.

String Beans with Potatoes 🍒

Tema

This is a vegetarian version of *Tema tang Sha*, page 74.

INGREDIENTS:

1 lb. string beans
2 large potatoes
$1/2$ small red pepper, thinly sliced
$1/2$ onion, chopped
1 tablespoon oil
2 cloves garlic, finely chopped
$1/2$ teaspoon paprika
1 inch fresh ginger, finely chopped
1 jalapeño chili, coarsely chopped
$1/2$ tomato, chopped
1 teaspoon soy sauce
salt to taste

Cut the string beans diagonally into $1^{1}/_{2}$-inch pieces. Cut the potatoes like French fries, about the same size as the beans. Slice the red pepper very thinly.

Sauté the onion in oil over high heat until softened, along with the garlic, paprika, and ginger. Add the potatoes, chili, and tomato, and stir-fry until the tomato cooks dry. Add the string beans and stir-fry till just tender, about 8–9 minutes. Add the soy sauce, red pepper, and salt, stirring in quickly.

Greens with Tofu 🍎

Tse Tofu

This very quick and easy dish also has lots of visual appeal, with the white tofu standing out against a background of dark green Swiss chard. Serve it with rice.

INGREDIENTS:

1 bunch Swiss chard
2 green onions, chopped
½ teaspoon paprika
2 cloves garlic, chopped
½ inch fresh ginger, chopped
2 tablespoons soy sauce
4 blocks firm tofu (12oz. each), cut into 1-inch cubes
¼ cup green peas
1 tablespoon oil
1 clove garlic, chopped
¼ teaspoon ground black pepper

Wash the Swiss chard and tear it into pieces, removing the stems.

Heat a little oil in a frying pan, and stir-fry green onions, along with the paprika, ginger, and 2 cloves of garlic. Stir in the soy sauce, tofu, and peas.

In a separate frying pan, heat a tablespoon of oil very hot. Stir in the black pepper. Add the Swiss chard, still slightly wet, and toss to coat with the oil and pepper. Cover the pan and let it steam for 30 seconds.

Spread the greens on a serving platter and pour the tofu mixture on top.

Bean Thread Noodles with Vegetables

Tse Ping

This is a quick and easy vegetarian version of the traditional *Ping Sha*, page 62, an auspicious dish served at weddings, Losar, and other celebrations.

Turmeric is sometimes added with the other spices, and Tibetans in India also add *garam masala*, but the results are less subtle.

INGREDIENTS:

3 medium waxy potatoes
4 oz. (2 bundles) bean thread noodles
½ cup dried wood ear fungus (optional)
½ onion, chopped
1 tomato, chopped
1 tablespoon vegetable oil
½ teaspoon paprika
½ inch fresh ginger, finely chopped
2 cloves garlic, finely chopped
¼ cup fresh or frozen green peas
¼ red bell pepper (optional)
¼ cup water

Cover the noodles in hot water, with room to expand, and leave them to soak for 20 minutes. In a separate bowl, pour boiling water to cover the dried fungus and soak for 20 minutes. Boil the potatoes until half cooked, rinse them in cold water, and slice them like French fries. Slice the bell pepper into thin strips. When the fungus has softened, cut it into 1-inch square pieces.

Sauté the onion in oil in a large pot until brown. Stir in the tomato. Chop the ginger and garlic finely and add them with the paprika, cooking briefly. Add the sliced potatoes and stir for one or two minutes. Add the peas, fungus, bell pepper, and water.

Drain the noodles. Chop the pile of noodles roughly into thirds and add them to the vegetable sauce.

Potatoes with Peas 🍎

Tse Shogo

This is a vegetarian version of *Shogo Ngopa*, page 69. Use the waxy type of potatoes for this dish. Baking potatoes will fall apart.

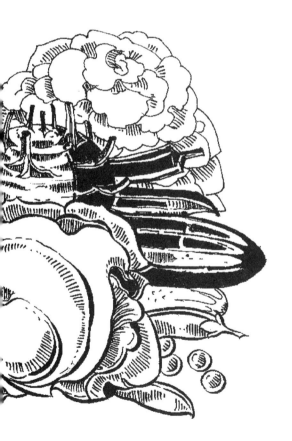

INGREDIENTS:

1 tablespoon oil
½ onion, coarsely chopped
2 cloves garlic, finely chopped
½ tomato, finely chopped
6 medium-small potatoes
½ cup fresh or frozen peas
1 tablespoon cilantro leaves, finely chopped

Boil the potatoes till just tender. Drain them and cut them in half lengthwise. Then slice them into half circles ⅓ inch thick.

Sauté the onion till translucent. Add the peas, tomato, and potatoes and stir-fry for one minute. Add 1 cup of warm water and heat through. Sprinkle the chopped cilantro on top just before serving.

Mushrooms with Mixed Vegetables

Tse Sesha

In Tibet, mushrooms are considered a substitute for meat. They are often used when meat is too expensive, and usually gathered wild in the fields, for free.

At least ten different varieties of mushroom are cultivated in Tibet. The common *kasha*, or "white mushroom" is similar to our ordinary field mushrooms. *Sesha*, or "yellow mushroom," is rarer and considered a delicacy. There is a Tibetan proverb, "On the farm, I can't leave *sesha* and go to *kasha*," or more loosely translated: "If I have steak at home why should I go out for hamburger?"

At Lhasa Moon, Tsering uses the oyster mushrooms available in Asian markets as a substitute for *sesha*. You might also try this with shitake for a special treat.

INGREDIENTS:

1 1/2 lbs. mushrooms
1 large carrot
2 tablespoons oil
2 cloves garlic, crushed
1/8 teaspoon ground black pepper
salt
1 clove garlic, chopped
1 lb. broccoli, cut into florets
1/2 red pepper, cut into 1-inch pieces

Cut the mushrooms in half if small, or slice them in thirds if they are larger. Don't slice them too thin or they will get mushy. Cut the carrot into 1-inch lengths and then cut vertically into square slices about 1/4 inch thick. Cut up the remaining vegetables.

In a wide, flat pan, fry the mushrooms over high heat with the garlic, black pepper, and salt, until they just begin to brown.

Coat a second pan with a little oil, and heat till very hot. Add the carrots, broccoli, and red pepper and stir-fry for one minute. Cover the pan and let it steam for another minute. Stir in the mushrooms and serve.

Vegetable Rainbow 🌱

Tse Nenzom

A variety of brightly colored vegetables are layered in a glass bowl for a visually appealing presentation.

This is a simplified version of a technique sometimes used for special occasions, where various cooked vegetables, as well as tofu, are arranged in a bowl and then steamed. The bowl is then inverted to serve the molded vegetables. Using a glass bowl shows the colors off in a similar way without cooking the vegetables a second time.

INGREDIENTS:

1 bunch spinach or ½ bunch Swiss chard
½ cabbage
½ lb. small mushrooms
2 carrots
¼ lb. snow peas
1 head broccoli
2 small yellow zucchini (optional)
oil for frying
1 tablespoon garlic, chopped
salt

Chop the spinach or Swiss chard coarsely. Cut the cabbage into 1-inch cubes. Cut each mushroom in half. Cut the carrots into thin slices lengthwise, and then into rectangles 1½ inches long. Cut the broccoli into florets and the zucchini into diagonal slices.

Use a small amount of oil in a very hot pan, with a little of the garlic and salt, to fry each vegetable separately. As each is cooked, spread it in a glass serving bowl, building layers up.

Vegetarian Cabbage Stir-fry 🍒

Logo Petse

This is a meatless version of the traditional *Logo Petse*, page 78.

INGREDIENTS:

1 tablespoon oil
½ onion, chopped
1 teaspoon paprika
2 cloves garlic, finely chopped
1 inch fresh ginger, finely chopped
1 tomato, chopped
2 carrots
½ head cabbage
1 red bell pepper

Prepare all the vegetables so you can add them quickly as you stir-fry. Cut the carrots and the bell pepper into julienne strips, about ⅛-inch thick. Cut the cabbage into ¼-inch slices.

Fry the onion over high heat with the paprika, garlic, and ginger till beginning to brown. Stir in the tomato and stir-fry briefly. Add carrots and stir-fry for 1 minute. Place the cabbage slices on top of the mixture without stirring, cover tightly and continue cooking for one minute only. Stir in the bell pepper slices and serve immediately.

Vegetable Curry 🐦

Tse Gyakar

Tsering invented this dish at Lhasa Moon to provide more vegetarian choices. It is a Tibetan interpretation of an Indian style of cooking vegetables. This is very good served with plain rice, or with Indian bread. Make the sauce more liquid if serving with rice.

INGREDIENTS:

2 carrots
1 small cauliflower
3 potatoes
1 tablespoon oil
3 large onions, cut into chunks
1 cinnamon stick
1 star anise
5 cloves
2–3 bay leaves
4 tomatoes, cut into quarters
1/4 cup peas
1 block tofu (12 oz.), cut into 1-inch cubes

Cut the carrots into 1-inch lengths and then into square slices 1/2 inch thick. Cut the cauliflower into small florets. Blanche the carrots and cauliflower for 2 minutes in boiling water, then drain. Cut the potatoes into quarters and then each quarter into 3 pieces. Boil the potatoes until just tender, then drain.

Sauté the onions with the spices until brown. Add the tomatoes and stir-fry until they cook down and the mixture begins to dry slightly. Stir in the cauliflower, carrots, and potatoes. Add water (1/2 to 1 cup) until the sauce is of the desired consistency. Add the peas and tofu and stir till heated through.

Eggplant with Potatoes 🍃

Duluma Tse

This dish adapts the traditional Tibetan method of cooking vegetables, in a spicy sauce of tomato and onion, to a new vegetable that the refugees encountered in India: eggplant. The result is especially good served with plain rice.

INGREDIENTS:

1 tablespoon oil
1 onion, chopped
1 inch fresh ginger, finely chopped
3 cloves garlic, finely chopped
1 tomato, chopped
1 large eggplant, or 6 small Japanese eggplant
3–4 potatoes

Sauté the onion, ginger, and garlic in oil until lightly browned. Add the tomato and cook until it begins to dry.

Slice the eggplant into thin, diagonal ovals if using the smaller Japanese eggplant, or thin semicircles for the larger eggplant. Cut the potatoes into thin slices of a similar size and shape. Wash the eggplant slices in water and add them to the tomato and onion mixture. Stir in the potatoes immediately. Cover tightly and cook over medium-low heat for 10 to 15 minutes. The water from the eggplant should be adequate to steam the potatoes, but if your lid does not fit tightly, you may need to add another ¼ cup of water.

Breads and Tsampa

The barley that is the staple food for most Tibetans does not contain enough gluten to make bread, and is therefore eaten as *tsampa,* a flour ground from the roasted grain and mixed with a little tea to make a stiff dough or a more liquid porridge.

A wide variety of breads are made from leavened wheat flour. They may be steamed or fried, baked on a griddle or in a covered pot, or buried in the hot ashes of a wood-burning stove. Modern ovens are not used in Tibet, nor in the settlements in India.

Rolling pins also are not used in Tibet, and all the shaping of bread, pasta, and pastry is done by patting the dough between the palms.

Flat Bread 🐾

Paley

This simple flat bread cooked on the stove top is good for soaking up sauces. It is as much a staple for the Tibetans raised in India as *tsampa* is for those from Tibet. Served with tea, and very good for dunking, it is the normal breakfast at the Tibetan monasteries in India. Sera Monastery is famous for its *paley,* a slightly sweet variation of the standard.

INGREDIENTS:

2½ cups flour
1 teaspoon dry yeast
½ teaspoon baking powder
1 cup water

Measure the flour into a large mixing bowl. Make a well in the center of the flour and place the yeast and baking powder inside. Add the water and mix well. Knead the dough until elastic. Cover it and let it sit for at least 45 minutes in a warm place, until doubled in size.

Divide the dough into four equal parts. Shape them by pressing between your hands into flat rounds about ¼ inch thick.

Heat a griddle or frying pan very hot, without oil. Cook the bread for 1 minute on each side, turning over a second time to cook a bit longer if necessary. Press a finger in the center of the bread to test. The bread will rise back if done, or retain a depression if not.

Hollow Bread 🍎

(Loko Momo)

Loko Momo are curious, igloo-shaped cups of bread that are both fried and steamed like pot-stickers.

INGREDIENTS:

2½ cups flour
1 teaspoon dry yeast
½ teaspoon baking powder
1 cup water
1 tablespoon oil
1 cup slightly salted water

Make a well in the center of the flour and place the yeast and baking powder inside. Add the water and mix well. Knead the dough until elastic. Cover it and let it sit for at least 45 minutes in a warm place, until doubled in size.

Divide the dough into four equal parts. Shape one portion into an igloo shape by pushing your thumbs into the center. The walls should be about ½ inch thick, slightly thinner on top.

Heat the oil in a frying pan over medium heat. Fry the first igloo shape, placing it in the center of the pan like an upside-down cup. Shape the remaining portions of dough, and add each one to the pan as soon as you have shaped it. Place each new *Loko Momo* in the center of the pan, moving the previously made ones to the edge.

When all four have browned on the bottom edge, turn the heat up high. Holding a tight-fitting lid tilted so that the steam will rise away from you, stand back, add the cup of salted water to the pan, and cover it immediately. The water will boil up suddenly. The *Loko Momos* should be done when the water boils dry, but you may need to add a little extra water. Press a finger into the bread to test it. It will rise back if done, or keep a depression if not.

Steamed Bread 🍐

Tingmo

Tingmo is a steamed bun, shaped like a cinnamon roll. They are usually made quite plain, or perhaps brushed with a little turmeric for color. At Lhasa Moon, Tsering adds garlic, which is not traditional.

INGREDIENTS:

2½ cups flour

1 teaspoon dry yeast

½ teaspoon baking powder

1 cup water

1 tablespoon melted butter or oil

¼ teaspoon turmeric (optional)

1 teaspoon garlic, finely chopped (optional)

Measure the flour into a large mixing bowl. Make a well in the center of the flour and place the yeast and baking powder inside. Add the water and mix well. Knead the dough until elastic. Cover it and let it sit for at least 45 minutes in a warm place, until doubled in size.

Roll the dough out on a floured surface to form a rectangle ¼ inch thick. If you are using turmeric, mix it into the melted butter or oil. Brush the butter evenly onto the dough and sprinkle with garlic, if you like. Make sure that the surface is completely covered across the width. Roll the dough up lengthwise and cut it with a sharp knife into slices 2 inches thick.

Place the slices, cut side up, in a steamer tray and steam for 10 minutes.

Amdo Bread 🍒

Amdo Paley

This pot-baked bread with a hard crust and fluffy interior originates in the Amdo region where His Holiness the Dalai Lama was born, and it is a favorite of his.

Sometimes *Amdo Paley* is filled with meat like a large stuffed *Sha Paley* (page 45). In that case, the dough is divided in two portions and a cooked meat filling spread between them. The edges are then pinched together and it is baked in the pot as usual.

INGREDIENTS:

2½ cups flour
1 teaspoon dry yeast
½ teaspoon baking powder
1 cup water

Measure the flour into a large mixing bowl. Make a well in the center of the flour and place the yeast and baking powder in it. Add the water gradually and mix well. Knead the dough and let it sit at least 45 minutes in a warm place, till doubled in size.

On a lightly floured surface, roll the dough out into a circle about 2 inches thick. The dough circle should just fit in the bottom of the pot you are using.

Heat a thick-bottomed pot with high sides. Brush the bottom and sides with oil. Place the dough circle in the pot and cover it. Turn the heat to low and cook for 20–30 minutes. When the top of the dough begins to get dry and hard, check the bottom. When the bottom has browned, turn the bread upside down and cook for 20 minutes more.

Remove the bread from the pot and cut it in wedges to serve.

Pancakes 🍒

Alla

Alla is a very simple, plain pancake made without eggs. It is easy to make on a campfire, and so popular when traveling. *Alla* also packs well for a lunch when working in the fields, or a picnic meal for initiations and teachings. This amount makes about 6 pancakes.

INGREDIENTS:

2 cups flour
1 teaspoon baking powder
2 cups water

Mix the ingredients, beating them thoroughly. Allow the batter to sit for at least half an hour, or better, overnight.

Heat a nonstick omelet pan over low to medium heat and brush it lightly with oil. When the pan is hot, immediately pour in about ¾ cup of the batter. Cook like a pancake. It is ready to turn over when holes form on the uncooked surface and the surface begins to dry. Cook until golden brown on both sides.

Parched Barley Flour 🍒

Tsampa

Barley is the staple food of Tibet, the hardiest of all grains and best suited to the country's high altitude and short growing season. It is prepared by first soaking the barley grains in water, and then roasting them, mixed with hot sand, over a fire. The sand, which distributes the heat evenly, is then sifted out and the roasted barley is ground into a fine flour. If you make *tsampa* in small batches, you don't need to bother with the sand.

Because the barley flour is precooked, the actual preparation for a meal is minimal. The *tsampa* is generally mixed with a little tea in one's own bowl, at the table, to make a stiff dough or a more liquid porridge, very good for breakfast. It is also used in cooking *Tsampa Tukpa*, page 60, a heavy soup with meat added to the basic porridge, and it is sometimes added to sweet dishes.

Being so simple to prepare, easy to carry, high in carbohydrates, and very warming, *tsampa* makes an excellent food for camping and backpacking.

Basic Tsampa Flour

Soak 1 lb. barley overnight in enough warm water to cover, allowing for expansion. Drain the barley and spread it out in a thin layer to dry on a cloth towel or trays lined with several layers of paper towels.

When the barley is still a little damp but not wet, thoroughly heat a large frying pan over very high heat. Turn the heat down to medium, and add ¼ of the barley. Cook the barley in four separate batches, stirring constantly. It is done when the grain is golden brown and makes gravelly noises as you stir it.

Cool the roasted barley completely. Grind it in small batches in a coffee grinder. Store in an airtight container.

Tsampa Dough (Pa)

The most common method of eating *tsampa* is to make a dough, called *pa*, in your own bowl. Simply take a cupful of *tsampa* in a small bowl, make a well in the middle, and pour in a little buttered tea (page 108). Use your fingers to brush the *tsampa* into the center gradually in a circular motion, kneading it in one hand to make a dough that is very firm and just wet enough not to crumble. If you would like to try this without the trouble of making buttered tea, use a little water, or ordinary black tea, and as much butter as you like. A little sugar or honey can be added for a treat, in which case the result is much like eating raw cookie dough.

To eat *pa*, break off lumps and pop them in your mouth. Or, squeeze a handful in your fist, pressing your thumb into the middle to make a hollow for spooning up soup or sauce.

> *A beggar calls to a child: "Give me one handful of* pa *and I'll tell you an interesting story. Give me two handfuls of* pa *and I'll tell you two interesting stories."*

Tsampa Porridge (Chamdu)

Another approach to eating tsampa is to make it into an instant porridge, called *chamdu*. Half fill an individual bowl with *tsampa* flour. Add 1 teaspoon of butter, and pour enough buttered tea (or black tea, hot water, or hot milk) over it to fill the bowl. Stir to mix the *tsampa* into the liquid, and add salt or sugar to taste.

For a more elaborate *chamdu* experience, half fill your bowl with *tsampa*, and then very gently pour in just enough buttered tea to cover the flour. Drink off the tea and lick the layer of wet *tsampa*. Then pour in some more tea and repeat the process until you finish the whole bowl. This method is said to be for old people who don't have to work but can sit in bed, half covered by blankets, with a teapot on a brazier beside the pillow, praying and drinking *chamdu* the whole day long.

Sweets and Desserts

Desserts are not eaten in Tibet as the conclusion to a meal, though sweet snacks are enjoyed and may be offered to guests before a meal. A substantial sweet dish can also be included as part of the main meal, especially at times when meat is avoided.

Many of the sweets, like *Desi* and *Kapseh,* are auspicious. They are served on ceremonial occasions and their ritual function as offerings or as vehicles of blessings and good luck is more important than their enjoyment as food.

Sweet Buttered Rice ❦

Desi

Desi is an auspicious ceremonial dish, traditionally eaten at weddings and on the first day of the new year. In Dharamsala, His Holiness the Dalai Lama gives teachings very early in the morning on this day. Hours before dawn, people bring their *desi* to Namgyal Monastery to be blessed by His Holiness.

The *droma* root, auspicious in itself, is gathered from the wild in Tibet. It is hard to come by even in Dharamsala. You can omit it entirely, or substitute sweet potato, which has a similar flavor. Use only the very best fragrant rice for this dish.

Desi should be served individually in small bowls, mounded high to signify prosperity.

INGREDIENTS:

2 cups basmati rice
¼ cup butter
1 handful dried *droma* or 1 small sweet potato
¼ cup yellow raisins
¼ cup sugar

Wash the rice and place it in a pot with 4 cups of water. Bring it to a boil, stir once, turn the heat down low and cover the pot. Let it cook till the water is absorbed, about 20 minutes.

Meanwhile, soak the raisins in cold water for 10 minutes. In another pot boil the *droma* or sweet potato, without peeling, till just cooked. It should not be soft or mushy. Remove it from the water and cut the *droma* into small pieces, or the sweet potato into ½-inch cubes.

When the rice has finished cooking, add the butter. Stir to fluff up the rice and mix in the melted butter. Stir in the raisins and sugar. Finally add the *droma* or sweet potato and toss very lightly to mix.

Caramel Cheese Pasta 🍎

Patsa Maku

Patsa Maku is an outrageously rich dish of fresh pasta topped with a sauce of caramelized sugar and cheese, and dripping with butter. It is traditionally served as a main course during Saka Dawa, the month-long celebration of the Buddha's birth and *parinirvana*. Many Tibetans avoid meat and fast on alternate days during this time, especially between the tenth and fifteenth days of the month. The fasting days are spent in prayer, often with the heavy exertion of continuous prostrations, so people fuel up with rich food on the alternate days.

At Lhasa Moon, Tsering has created a lighter variation of *Patsa Maku* that still delivers the unique flavor combination of cheese and caramelized sugar. Instead of fresh pasta, she uses small steamed rolls. The little spiral buns coated in sauce are also more visually appealing than the traditional *Patsa Maku*.

Traditional Patsa Maku

The fresh pasta is formed by hand into small curls that look like little shells and hold the sauce well.

PASTA INGREDIENTS:

2 cups flour
1 1/2 cups water (approximately)

SAUCE INGREDIENTS:

1 cup butter
3/4 cup fresh *Chuship* cheese, page 116, or substitute
    1/2 cup ricotta and 1/4 cup grated parmesan
1/2 cup light brown sugar

Mix the flour and water together to make a stiff dough. The amount of water needed will vary with the type and age of the flour used, so mix in 1 cup of water first and add more gradually as needed. Knead the dough till very elastic. Cover it and let it rest for 1/2 hour.

On a well-floured surface, roll or pat the dough into a round 3/4 inch thick and cut it into thin strips with a sharp knife. Roll each strip between two hands till it is as thin as your little finger. Tear the strips into half-inch pieces. Rub each piece in a curling motion with your thumb against the palm of the other hand to make small hollow shell shapes. Bring a large pot of water to the boil and add the pasta all at once. Boil for 2–3 minutes, stirring constantly. Pour through a strainer to drain.

While the water is boiling, melt the butter in a saucepan over low heat. Add the hot drained pasta, cheese, and brown sugar. Stir together quickly and lightly until the cheese and sugar have melted. Serve hot.

Tsering's Patsa Maku (Caramel Cheese Rolls)

PASTRY INGREDIENTS:

2 cups flour
1 1/2 cups water (approximately)
1 tablespoon dry yeast
1 teaspoon baking powder
1 tablespoon butter, softened
1 tablespoon brown sugar
2 tablespoons parmesan cheese
1 tablespoon *tsampa* (optional)

SAUCE INGREDIENTS:

1/2 pint heavy cream
1 cup light brown sugar

Dissolve yeast in 1 cup warm water. Add baking powder and flour and mix well. Add more water as needed to make a fairly soft dough and knead till elastic. Cover the dough and let it sit in a warm place for an hour to rise.

On a floured board, roll the dough out to a rectangle 1/2 inch thick. Spread the butter to cover the dough completely. Sprinkle the brown sugar, parmesan cheese, and *tsampa* evenly over the dough. (The *tsampa* adds a subtle, distinctive flavor but can be omitted.) Roll the dough into a long log and cut into 1-inch slices with a sharp knife. Arrange the rolls in a steamer with space between them, and steam for 4 minutes.

Mix the cream and sugar in a small saucepan over low heat. Stir constantly, letting it boil for about 3 minutes after the sugar is dissolved. The sauce should caramelize, turning brown slightly. Place the steamed buns on a plate and pour the sauce over them.

Sweet Cheese Dumplings 🍒

Minya Polo

These are essentially sweet *momos*, with a filling that resembles rich cookie dough. Like *Patsa Maku*, *Minya Polo* is not really a dessert, but is served as a snack or a sweet main course during the month of Saka Dawa. It is made almost exclusively in the households of the Lhasa aristocracy.

The sugar normally used for this is grated from lumps of palm sugar imported from India. Dark brown sugar is a reasonable substitute.

If you like the idea of sweet *momos*, you might want to experiment with other fillings. Apple or other fruit pie fillings would work well.

INGREDIENTS:

2½ cups flour
¾ cup water
1 cup *Tsampa*, page 95
½ cup *Chuship*, page 116, or finely grated parmesan cheese
½ cup butter, melted
½ cup brown sugar

Mix the flour and water into dough, and knead it well. The amount of water needed may vary slightly depending on the flour. The dough should be as moist as for ordinary bread. Cover the dough and set it aside to rest while preparing the filling.

Use your fingers to mix the *tsampa* flour, cheese, butter and sugar together until evenly blended.

Shape the dough and fill it just as for *Momos*, page 37, making round shapes only. Steam the filled pastries for 5–7 minutes.

Festive Fried Pastries 🦂

Kapseh

A familiar sight on the family altar at the new year is the offering of *kapseh* pastries and other fried dough shapes, stacked in a high tower and decorated with dried apricots, cheese, dates, nuts, and candies. *Kapseh* also make an appearance at weddings and many other ritual celebrations.

They are made in vast amounts in the monasteries for special teachings and prayer sessions, and placed on the shrine during the ceremony along with other food offerings. Having gathered the power of the prayers and mantras said all day, the pastries are distributed by the monks to the people after the ceremony. They are taken home to share with those who could not attend the ceremony, fed to the family's dogs and cattle, or spread on the farm land. The monastery *kapseh* are not very appetizing. In fact they are quite tough and tasteless, made quickly in bulk using very little sugar or butter. If you have ever been blessed with one of these tough, tasteless sticks of greasy dough, don't let them prejudice your opinion of all *kapseh*.

Making *kapseh* at home for Losar often begins a month before the new year, as the pastries keep well in the dry climate. It is a major operation and the family works as an assembly line, rolling the dough, cutting the shapes, watching the pot and turning the pieces as they fry. The very first shape to be made is a small scorpion sculpted of dough, which serves as a test for the oil temperature and then sits on top of the stove to ward off negativity.

The amounts given below will make enough to serve a large group, as the pastries are very rich. Clarified butter (ghee) is the best oil for frying *kapseh*, especially if you really intend to eat them, but any neutral vegetable oil works well enough.

INGREDIENTS:

oil for deep frying
4 cups flour
½ cup melted butter
1 cup sugar
½ cup water
powdered sugar (optional)

Measure the flour into a large mixing bowl. Make a well in the flour and pour the melted butter into it. Pour the sugar on top and mix well with your hands. Add water gradually until the dough is as moist as a firm cookie dough. Knead it well.

Divide the dough into three parts and work with one at a time. Roll the dough into a smooth ball between your palms, and then roll it out into a flat sheet ½ inch thick. You should need only minimal flour to prevent the dough from sticking. Cut the dough into the traditional shapes.

Simple Kapseh Shape

Cut a rectangle or lozenge shape about 3 inches by 1 inch with a slit down the middle.

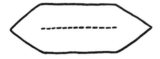

Insert one end through the slit and pull gently to extend.

"Eternal Knot" Kapseh

This kapseh shape represents the eternal knot, an auspicious symbol for the Buddha's infinite wisdom.

Cut a rectangle about 3 inches by 4 inches with seven slits across the middle.

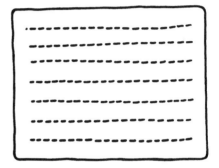

Pinch the sides together to form a tube and lay the seam underneath.

Pinch the top strip of dough in the center, and pull straight up.

Pinch the next strips, pulling alternately to left and right.

Heat the oil in a deep pan till hot, turning the heat to medium before adding the dough shapes. Add a few at a time, so that they are not more than a single layer deep in the oil. The *kapseh* will bubble and rise to the surface, but should not brown too fast. When they are golden, remove them from the oil and drain them in a strainer or on paper towels.

If you like, sprinkle the *kapseh* with powdered sugar while still very hot so the sugar sticks to the surface. With or without sugar, don't stack them on top of each other until they are completely cool.

Extra Special Festive Fried Pastries

Sanga Paley

This is a richer, more refined version of *Kapseh* that is made in the homes of aristocratic families on special occasions. You can make an especially fine version of *Sanga Paley* by using prepared filo pastry instead of the normal *Kapseh* dough.

INGREDIENTS:

oil for deep frying
4 cups flour
½ cup melted butter
1 cup sugar
½ cup water
powdered sugar

Follow the directions for making *Kapseh* dough, page 102, but roll the dough out as thinly as possible. Ideally it should be paper thin.

Cut the dough into rectangles, about 2½ by 4 inches. Brush each one with additional melted butter. Stack the rectangles six or seven layers deep if you have managed to roll the dough paper thin, or just four layers if it is slightly thicker.

Seal the edges of the short sides of each rectangle by pinching them, working down the edge and folding a little bit over with each pinch to make a spiral pattern. Then make three deep cuts lengthwise through the center of each rectangle.

Deep fry the *Sanga Paley* according to the directions for *Kapseh,* page 104, adding powdered sugar while the pastries are still very hot.

Beverages

Don't say that someone who drinks
is lacking in education.
The melodies, the beautiful songs,
the dances that they offer
are their own erudition.
—*Tibetan drinking song*

Buttered Tea 🍂

Poecha

The infamous Tibetan buttered tea is not so much an acquired taste as it is a different approach to the whole matter of drinking tea. The slightly salty, broth-like concoction is consumed in large amounts as people sip it all day to keep warm and avoid dehydration in the high altitude. The tea is actually quite weak, and the salt probably provides a correct electrolyte balance. (Although Tibetans in exile have become fond of the stronger, sweetened Indian tea, they acknowledge sadly that one can't drink more than three cups at a time.)

A large leaf tea is imported from China, and was also grown in eastern Tibet. It is a fermented black tea pressed into hard, dry cakes, either rectangular or cup-shaped. You can buy a similar variety in Chinese markets in this country under the name of *bo nay* tea. (A warning: other Chinese compressed teas such as *pu erh beeng cha* have a completely different flavor.) The compressed tea is boiled for 20 minutes, but does not produce the bitter taste that you normally get from boiling black tea. You can make a reasonable facsimile of Tibetan tea using any plain black tea such as Lipton's, but it should be steeped rather than boiled.

The added butter is better suited to cold high altitudes than conditions in exile, and you will probably want to use much less than would be appreciated in Tibet. There, adding too little is a sign of cheapness or disrespect to guests. (Leaving it out altogether won't do: the very poorest Tibetans in India will sometimes use oil instead of butter.)

The traditional tea churn is a tall wooden cylinder, decorated with brass and fitted with a wooden plunger. The churning is necessary to distribute the butter evenly in the liquid so each person gets an equal share. Otherwise the butter will rise to the top. It does eventually anyway, as the churning does not quite emulsify it totally, but at least it stays suspended for long enough to pour it. A plastic churn has become popular with Tibetans in the West, but a blender also works well.

Once the tea is in your cup, you can blow on the surface to cool it and make the butter solidify in a layer on top. You can use this trick to avoid drinking the butter when your hosts are too generous. Or, you can do as the Tibetans do and mix a little *tsampa* into the butter that remains stuck to the bottom and sides of the cup, eating it like cookie dough.

INGREDIENTS:

⅓ cup compressed tea or 4 black tea bags
1½ cups milk
2–4 tablespoons butter
¾ teaspoon salt

If you are using tea bags, pour 2 cups of boiling water over them and leave them to steep for 5 minutes. If you are using compressed tea, add it to 3 cups of water in a small saucepan and boil gently for 20 minutes, stirring occasionally to separate the tea leaves. Strain the boiled tea (which should have reduced to about 2 cups) or remove the tea bags.

Add the milk, butter, and salt to the concentrated tea. Boil up a separate kettle full of water. Pour roughly ⅓ of the concentrated tea mixture into a blender. Add 2⅓ cups boiling water, blend briefly, and serve immediately. Repeat for two more batches, till you have used all the tea concentrate and a total of 7 cups of boiling water. You may want to wait to blend the second or third batch until you are ready to serve refills.

Sweet Yogurt Shake 🐚

Tara

Traditionally, *tara* was simply buttermilk, but now the influence of sweet Indian *lasi* has changed the drink in the exile communities.

INGREDIENTS:

4 cups (2 lbs.) plain yogurt
10 ice cubes
½ cup brown sugar

Blend the ingredients together in a blender until smooth.

Spiced Tea 🐚

Chai

The Indian *chai masala* has become very popular amongst Tibetans in the refugee communities, and is healthier in the Indian climate than the traditional buttered tea.

INGREDIENTS:

4 cups cold water
4 cardamom pods
1 inch fresh ginger, crushed
2 black tea bags
1 cup whole milk
1 tablespoon sugar

Crush the cardamom pods and ginger and add them to the cold water. Slowly bring the water to a boil. Remove from the heat and add the tea bags. Allow the mixture to sit for several minutes. Remove the tea bags and add the milk and sugar. Reheat and serve.

Barley Beer 🍇

Chang

Home brewed barley beer is extremely popular amongst Tibetans. For many it is a daily staple, watered down for children, and it is indispensable at parties and celebrations. The slightly effervescent, pale milky brew has a tangy flavor and a deceptively light alcohol content that can easily tempt one to over-indulge.

The first bowl of *chang* to be poured is placed as an offering at the family's shrine. Likewise, the first taste of your own bowl is given as an offering to the Three Jewels, with the ring finger of the left hand dipped lightly into the liquid and flicked off the thumb three times, for the Buddha, Dharma, and Sangha. A host will be offended unless you drink more than one bowl, and preferably three, but you can minimize the damage by drinking just a few sips before allowing your bowl to be refilled.

The enjoyment of *chang* is not complete without at least one drinking song. A Tibetan drinking song does not at all imply what the term means in the West, but is a much more delicate communication with its own special etiquette. The hostess might begin to sing as she first pours the *chang* for her guests, in much the same spirit as one would offer a toast. She continues the song as they make an offering of the first taste and drink a sip, continuing still as she tops up the bowls and the guests drink a second and again a third time, finally giving a "bottoms up" signal as she approaches the end of the song. (Once it's in your hands, never put the bowl down as long as the singing continues! If you finish your bowl too soon, or leave anything in it at the end, you will be punished with yet another refill.)

The melodies of the drinking songs are traditional, but the singer will ideally improvise the lyrics on the spot to suit the moment. It might be a love song, or contain some other message, but it is always addressed by the singer to someone present. If the recipient is alert and gets the message, he or she will sing another song in reply. When Tsering returns to the settlement at Bylakuppe to visit her family, her mother offers a *chang* song to welcome her home, and another, sadder one at the goodbye party on her departure:

The time I spent with you went like the wind;
I don't know how my time will pass when you're not here.

This recipe makes a large bucket full of *chang*, enough for a good party. Barley is most often used, but the same method also works well with white or brown rice.

INGREDIENTS:

5 lbs. barley or rice

5½ quarts water

½ cup active dry baker's yeast

The second batch of *chang* will be much weaker than the first. You can blend the two together before serving, or offer a choice of both separately. The *chang* will keep 2–3 days.

Boil the grain in water over gentle heat, covered, until it has absorbed all the liquid, much like you would make rice normally. Depending on the size of your cooking pot you may have to do this in batches.

Spread the cooked grain out on a clean cloth or on cookie sheets to cool. When it is lukewarm, sprinkle the yeast over it. Mix the yeast well into the grain. (If you have spread it on cloth, two people can hold each end and toss it together.)

Put the mixture immediately into a large strong plastic garbage bag, and place the bag inside a second bag. Place the garbage bag inside a sleeping bag and wrap it well. Keep it in a warm room but away from direct sunlight for at least one week. At this point the *chang* is said to be "sleeping" and the longer it sleeps the better. Left to sleep for a year it will be very strong indeed.

On the day you intend to serve it, transfer the mash to a large pot. Cover it with water to about 2 inches above the level of the grain. Let it sit for 2 hours, and then strain it through a cheesecloth into another container. Return the mash to the pot and cover it again with the same amount of fresh water. Let it sit for 2 hours and strain again.

Mulled Barley Beer 🍐

Chang Kue

Chang kue is a special Losar treat. On the first day of the new year, Tsering's parents would rise at around 3:00 in the morning. After washing and dressing in new clothes, her mother brought each member of the family a bowl of hot *chang kue*, served as breakfast in bed. A mother's greeting of *"tashi delek"* is the first thing a child should hear on waking to the new year. The children would rush out to set off fire crackers and then go back to bed for a few more hours while their parents made offerings and prayed.

Chang kue is made from the fermented mash that is the basis for *chang*, except that it is usually made with rice instead of barley. This recipe makes enough for four people. If you don't have the dried cheese called *churkam*, simply leave it out.

INGREDIENTS:

2 cups fermented rice mash (see instructions for *Chang*, page 112)
3 cups water
¼ cup raisins
⅓ cup *Churkam*, page 117
¼ cup *Tsampa* flour, page 95

Mix the rice mash with water in a saucepan and bring to the boil. Add the raisins, cheese, and *tsampa* flour. Boil the mixture until it thickens very slightly. It should be quite liquid; add more water if it is too thick. Serve hot.

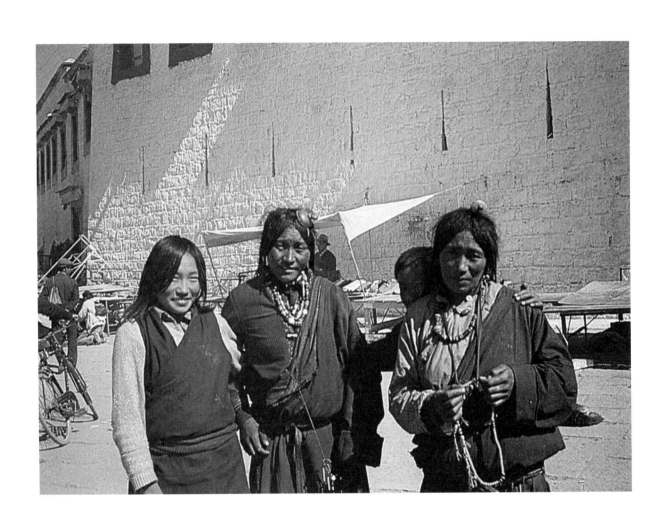

CHEESES

As you might expect in a culture where most families will keep at least a few animals for milk, making cheese is a household affair. The *dri* (female yak) and the hybrid *dzo*, which are the favored milk-cows in Tibet, produce a much richer milk than whole cows' milk. But the cheeses included here can be made satisfactorily with ordinary cows' milk, or even with low fat or nonfat milk.

Fresh Cheese 🌸

Chuship

This works best with yogurt that does not have added thickeners or stabilizers. Whole milk yogurt makes a deliciously rich cheese, but nonfat yogurt works well enough.

INGREDIENTS:

2 teaspoons sugar
4 cups plain yogurt (2 lbs.)

Mix the sugar with the yogurt and bring to a boil over medium heat. Boil for several minutes, until the curds begin to separate from the clear whey. (If the yogurt has added stabilizers it will get lumpy but not separate clearly.)

Pour the boiled yogurt into a strainer lined with several layers of cheese cloth, or a large paper coffee filter. Let it drain for a few hours.

Squeeze the cheese in your fist to form small, crumbly lumps. Spread it on a plate and leave it in a cool place or in the refrigerator to dry out for a day or two. Then store in an air-tight container in the refrigerator. It will keep for at least a week.

Fresh *chuship* is used in desserts such as Caramel Cheese Pasta (*Patsa Maku*), page 99, and Sweet Cheese Dumplings (*Minya Polo*), page 101. It is also good in Spinach and Cheese *Momos*, page 44.

Dried Cheese ❦

Churkam

You can chew on this rock-hard, slightly sweet cheese for hours, like chewing gum. It's a treat for children and a favorite snack for travelers, as it fills the time. Elderly people chew it to keep their gums and teeth in good shape.

Make a batch of fresh *Chuship*, page 116, using cheesecloth. After letting the cheese drain for a few hours, gather up the cheesecloth and tie the ends in a knot. Place the package on a plate with a heavy weight on top and leave it overnight.

Open the cheesecloth and cut the cheese into 1-inch cubes. Thread the cubes on a string, and hang them in a sunny place to dry for 7 to 10 days. *Churkam* will keep indefinitely—for centuries probably!

Ripened Cheese 🫐

Churu

Don't bother making this mold-ripened cheese if you get queasy about mysterious organisms or faint-hearted at the thought of science experiments in the kitchen. Blue cheese makes a perfectly good substitute in all the recipes in this book that call for *churu*.

Tsering recalls how the whole house would smell when her family made *churu*, which literally means "rotten cheese," at home in India. Sometimes the cheese would be full of worms, but could be saved by leaving it in the sunshine so the worms would crawl out. The process is probably less gruesome in the colder Tibetan climate.

INGREDIENTS:

4 cups plain yogurt (2 lbs.)
2 teaspoons sugar
1 teaspoon salt
2 tablespoons oil

Mix the yogurt with the sugar and bring to a boil over medium heat. Boil for several minutes, until the curds begin to separate from the clear whey. Pour the boiled yogurt into a strainer lined with several layers of cheese cloth, or a large paper coffee filter. Let it drain for a few hours.

Add the salt to the drained fresh cheese. Heat the oil over medium heat in a frying pan and add the cheese. Cook it, stirring frequently, until it turns yellowish. Let the mixture cool and then put it in a tightly covered container. It will start to smell after a few days. Leave it for at least a week before using, the longer the better. If the right type of mold has grown, other organisms won't compete with it. If you end up with the wrong growth, the cheese will taste foul. Eat this at your own risk, and only if it tastes like blue cheese!

CHILI SAUCES AND PICKLES (SIBEH)

Tibetan food is often very mildly seasoned but served with a fiery hot sauce on the side. The sauce may be as basic as a few chopped green chili peppers in a little soy sauce, or one of the more elaborate creations from the following pages.

There is a common belief amongst Tibetans that, in general, women prefer spicier food than men. We may not be aware of our own stereotypes in this matter: when we offered samples of a really fierce chili sauce for sale at a fundraiser for the Tibetan Opera Company, it was American men, by a great majority, who seemed to take the offer as a personal challenge.

Chili Sauce with Cheese 🍒

Churu Sibeh

The characteristic combination of hot chilies with mold-ripened cheese is unique to Tibetan cooking. You can make your own *Churu* (page 118) or use blue cheese as a substitute. There are two versions of *Churu Sibeh*, one using dried red chilies and one using fresh green ones. Both are equally good, and both keep well indefinitely if refrigerated.

Red Churu Sibeh

INGREDIENTS:

½ cup dried crushed red chili
1 teaspoon salt
4 cloves garlic
¼ cup blue cheese
1 cup water

For the best texture, grind the ingredients together in a large mortar and pestle, adding the water gradually at the end. Otherwise, grind everything together in a blender.

Green Churu Sibeh

INGREDIENTS:

1 onion, chopped
2 tablespoons oil
1–2 cloves garlic, chopped
1 teaspoon salt
1 tomato, chopped
½ lb. jalapeño chilies, cut into halves lengthwise
½ cup water
⅓ cup blue cheese

Remove the seeds from the chilies for a milder sauce, or leave them in for more heat. Sauté the onion in oil until it begins to brown. Add garlic and salt, and cook for a minute more. Add the tomato and chilies, stirring for a few minutes over high heat. Add the water and cheese. Lower the heat to medium and continue stirring until the cheese melts and the chilies turn soft.

Coriander Chili Sauce 🍒

Sonam Penzom Sibeh

There are two versions of this popular chili sauce, one with yogurt and one with tomato. The sauce does not keep for longer than a few days because the fresh cilantro loses flavor quickly.

INGREDIENTS:

1 bunch cilantro
4–5 small green chilies or 2 jalapeño chilies
½ cup dried crushed red chilies
1 cup yogurt or 1 large tomato
4–5 cloves garlic
1 teaspoon salt
½ cup water

Cut the cilantro into short lengths. If you are using tomato, cut it into quarters. Place all the ingredients together in a blender and blend until just uniform but still a little chunky.

Soaked Chilies 🐦

Sibeh Pang-ja

This method of preparing chili sauce is unique to the Kongpo region. It makes a very fiery thin liquid that you can serve as a dipping sauce with any kind of bread. It keeps indefinitely. I'm not sure if the heat of the chilies fades over time, or one rapidly develops a tolerance, but the result is addictive. When the liquid is finished, you can reuse the soaked chilies in cooking, or grind them up and use them again for another batch of *Sibeh Pang-ja*.

INGREDIENTS:

⅓ cup dried whole red chilies
1 teaspoon *Churu*, page 118, or blue cheese
2–4 cloves garlic, crushed
⅛ teaspoon whole *emma* (Sichuan pepper)
⅓ cup hot tea or hot water

Place all the ingredients in a small container. Cover it tightly and shake well. Let the mixture sit for a few hours, and shake again before serving.

Pickled Vegetables 🍎

Tangtse Nyipa

Tangtse nyipa translates literally as "sleeping vegetables." Pickled vegetables are especially popular amongst elderly Tibetans. Cabbage is often used, in which case the result is very similar to Korean kimchee. Daikon is another favorite, and is usually colored pink by the addition of beet root in the jar.

Pickled Cabbage

INGREDIENTS
1 small white cabbage
1 tablespoon salt
3–4 dried red chilies
¼ teaspoon whole *emma* (Sichuan pepper)

Cut the cabbage roughly into chunks about 1–2 inches square. Mix the cabbage well with the salt and spices.

Pack as tightly as possible into a wide-mouthed jar. Add just enough water to cover the cabbage. Cover the jar and leave in a warm place for at least five days.

Pickled Daikon

INGREDIENTS:
1 large daikon
1 tablespoon salt
3–4 dried red chilies
¼ teaspoon whole *emma* (Sichuan pepper)
1 slice beet root

Slice the daikon into thin rounds—the thinner the slices, the less time needed for fermentation. Toss the daikon slices with the salt and spices.

Place a slice of raw beet root in the bottom of a wide-mouthed jar. Pack the daikon slices tightly into the jar. Add just enough water to cover the vegetables. Cover the jar and leave in a warm place for at least five days.

ILLUSTRATION CREDITS

Drawings

Photographs